CURING CHRISTIANITY

OVERCOMING DOUBT, FEAR, *and* CONFUSION *to* REDISCOVER *a* HEALTHY CHRISTIAN FAITH

D.L. WEBSTER

Curing Christianity

Unless otherwise indicated, all Scripture quotations are taken from the Holy Bible, New International Version®, NIV®.

ISBN 979-8-9941851-0-0

Library of Congress Control Number: 2026905156

First Edition
Printed in the United States of America.

Cover design by Laura Powel – Studio 3886
Interior design by Evgeniia Gurcheva
Edited by Megan Tatreau and Kelley Matthews

Spherical Media and Publishing
Nashville, Tennessee

www.dlwebster.com

Note: In the stories shared in this book, names have been changed in order to maintain their anonymity.

CURING CHRISTIANITY

Contents

Preface

"Every good tree bears good fruit, but a bad tree bears bad fruit. A good tree cannot bear bad fruit, and a bad tree cannot bear good fruit ... Thus, by their fruit you will recognize them." Matthew 7:17–20

I have spent most of my life connected to evangelical Christian churches. Through this, I've had the pleasure of knowing many great believers. These people demonstrate sincere concern for others, often sacrificing their time and money to help others in need. They are passionate about following Jesus and the positive impact they believe his presence has in their life. They deeply desire for others to experience freedom and healing. They want to be a part of Christ's mission: "The blind receive sight, the lame walk, those who have leprosy are cleansed, the deaf hear, the dead are raised, and the good news is proclaimed to the poor" (Matt 11:5).

I have also heard the stories of those who have been hurt—or even traumatized—by Christianity. I have noticed a handful of practices and ideas that have caused people to doubt God's love, their faith, and to experience mental and emotional anguish. In this book, I will examine ten areas which have caused believers confusion or harm. At best, the problematic ideas and practices have left many believers with a less secure, less robust faith than they otherwise could have. At worst, these have led people to question their faith—"deconstruction"—if not leaving it altogether.

I want individual believers to have the healthiest faith possible. Likewise, I have a passion for Christianity collectively to be the best version of itself possible. This is why I have written this book. Over my years of experience, I have gained a solid grasp on Christianity. I want to share the insight God has granted me in order to strengthen both people's faith individually as well as to improve Christianity as a whole.

I believe that the problems that have tripped people up are not a core part of Christianity. I disagree with those who hold that a person can't be Christian if they do not understand Christianity in a certain way. Rather, problems come as a result of either misunderstanding or errant practice of the Christian faith.

The title *Curing Christianity* came first from the idea of solidifying one's faith—one of the goals of this book—similar to how concrete cures. But I love the double meaning of curing in relation to health. I want to heal problematic aspects of Christianity in order for it to become wholly healthy.

I originally considered titling this book *Correcting Christianity*. However, Jesus Christ doesn't need correcting, nor does Christianity, in so much as it is the concept of following Jesus's teachings. Yet, those of us who follow Jesus are not perfect. And it's we imperfect people who manifest Christianity in the world. When we drift away from the good news of Jesus—whether intentionally or not—we risk saying or doing things that can cause harm to others. When these harms happen, they are antithetical to the good news of Jesus. After all, harm and trauma aren't good news, are they?

For some people, to support, love, and cherish a person, group, or institution means to only speak good about that entity and never criticize it. Specifically for our discussion, there are Christians who believe that if anyone says anything besides preaching the Bible as these Christians understand it, then that person is undermining Christianity. But I believe that true love for a person, group, or institution leads to a desire for that entity to be the best it can be. This sometimes involves pointing out an aspect of, in this case, Christian beliefs or practices that have room for improvement.

Evangelicals believe all people should either become Christians if they are not already or remain Christians if they are. However, the problematic beliefs certain Christians hold unnecessarily have caused some to leave their faith while also presenting a barrier to others who might consider faith in Jesus. Christians should be interested in understanding these reasons as well as potential solutions.

The causes behind the harm and/or loss of faith are, I believe, blind spots to most Christians. In other words, I don't believe Christians are intentionally trying to harm others or lead to their loss of faith. I hope to reveal these blind spots, to demonstrate how they are not an integral part of Christianity, and to offer guidance in how to avoid these pitfalls.

As you read this book, I expect you will agree with a good portion of what I've written. However, you will likely find some things new and challenging. I hope you will keep an open mind while reading through the challenging parts. One of my paradigms is that a dead tree which is rigid is more likely to break than a living tree which bends in the wind. In other words, I suggest that a rigid understanding of Christianity is more prone to break (deconversion).

The good news is that your faith does not need to be brittle. God loves us and wants us to be spiritually healthy. More resilient faith awaits through these pages.

Existential Fear of the Boogeyman

"Do not give way to fear." 1 Peter 3:6

"'Do not call conspiracy everything this people calls a conspiracy; do not fear what they fear, and do not dread it.'" Isaiah 8:12, 1 Peter 3:14

Why would I start a book regarding Christianity with a chapter on fear? Fear may be the biggest, most unacknowledged sin prevalent among Christians today. More precisely, it's the actions people take as a result of fear which perhaps account for the most sin.

Fear itself isn't bad; it's how we choose to respond to fear that can be good or bad. A variety of feelings can be grouped under the general category of fear. You might be startled if someone jumps out from behind a corner, for example. Or you may feel terror if you see a bear cross your path as you hike. Many people have a fear of speaking in front of others. You might be afraid of failing on a project. Or you may worry if your child comes home late.

I'm not saying all of these are sin. Furthermore, fear is like anger—the emotion itself isn't wrong. We are human, and part of our humanity is feeling emotions. Our emotions are important signals that give us insight into ourselves and the world around us. They are like gauges that monitor how we are doing in ways we might not otherwise be aware of.

However, what our emotions tell us isn't always the true reality of our situation. We must evaluate our feelings in order to determine what message they are trying to send and if this message is accurate. God has given us our minds and intends us to use our reason in concert with our emotions in order to make wise choices (Rom 12:2, Jas 1:5, Phil 1:9–10).

For example, if our friends plan a surprise party for us, we might feel fear the moment everyone jumps out and yells, "Surprise!" In that moment, we might get a shot of adrenaline and our heart rate jumps. Our body is telling us, "Danger!" even though we are clearly safe. In this scenario, we should be able to quickly recognize our safety and react not by running out the door or by punching the nearest person in the face. However, not every situation is as clear, and our body doesn't always go along with our conscious thoughts right away. In other words, even if we consciously recognize we are safe in a particular situation, we may still physically feel fear, worry, nervousness, or anxiousness.

Fear affects your life personally. I can say this with confidence because it affects all of us. The question is, do you recognize the fears in your life? Can you determine which of your fears are unreasonable and choose to act despite them?

For years, when people talked about fear, I only thought of the feeling of being scared such what as I might experience in a haunted house. I didn't recognize how fear affected my life for a long time. I finally realized that I refrained from doing certain things because my unconscious mind thought that *if* I did them, *then* I would feel afraid. My unconscious mind tried to protect me from scary feelings by avoiding them before I even got to the point of feeling them consciously.

For example, one time I went to buy flowers for a friend of mine. Once at the store, I realized I felt hesitation to do so. I recognized this and began to ponder why I was apprehensive. I figured out that carrying flowers through the store would be noticeable, and I had buried memories of kids teasing others about boys "liking" girls. As a child, I had unconsciously developed a strategy of avoiding painful criticism by going unnoticed. Once I was able to understand this and realize my fear was unreasonable, I was able to choose to act despite my fear.

Fear triggers self-preservation instincts. This isn't bad. Just like the rest of the emotions God created us with, fear has a useful function. Being safe is good. God wants us to be alive and healthy, and the self-preservation instincts help us in this regard.

However, emotions aren't intelligent and aren't always right. Even when they are, the actions our feelings want us to take may not lead to the actions that God wants us to take. Our emotions are fallen like the rest of us.

A godly response to fear often goes against our natural instincts. For example, Jesus clearly—and very understandably—feared the experience of being tortured and crucified for our sins. He felt so distraught that he sweat blood immediately beforehand. Yet he chose to trust the Father and took the path of self-sacrifice for our sake.

It's clear from both Scripture and Jesus that God loves people. The Bible instructs us to love others, because we are to represent God's love in the world. The Bible says that, "God is love" and "perfect love drives out fear" (1 John 4:8, 16, 18).

The Bible also speaks about the fear of the Lord. I've heard many a Christian struggle to understand this concept. I have found it helpful to consider its opposite. What does it look like *not* to fear God? Those who don't consider God in their lives, who don't respect or take seriously his ways, do not practice the fear of God. In contrast, those who do fear God do recognize him and take seriously his ways. The fear of the Lord doesn't mean a person is terrified of God. Once again, "Perfect love drives out fear." Instead, fear of the Lord means that one takes seriously God and tries to live in his ways.

If fear motivated only positive or merely inconsequential behavior, then I wouldn't be writing this chapter. As it is, many of the actions we take as a result of fear lead us to act in ways contrary to the ways of Jesus. This shouldn't be surprising. In the Bible, people are instructed over eighty times, "Do not be afraid." And fear is mentioned in some way over five hundred times. Clearly, fear is a common human emotion. A decision to follow Christ doesn't immediately make a person perfect. God neither immediately removes our fears nor our natural reactions to fear. Recognizing our fears and learning to respond to them in a Christ like way is a part of learning to be disciple of Jesus.

Fear raises our defenses. We may attack the object of our fear in an attempt to eliminate it. If the object of our fear is a spider, then perhaps this isn't a big deal. But what if the object of our fear is our neighbor? The apostle Paul tells us that we fight not against other people but against spiritual forces. However, we often think *other people* are the enemy. God wants us to love others. I will examine love more thoroughly in the next chapter. But for now, understand that building walls to protect us from others or attacking them aren't ways of loving people.

I'm not arguing against prudence. Locking your door at night is prudent, for example. There are people in the world who will do harm if given the chance. I'm not saying that we love them by letting them take what they want or allowing them to inflict harm. God may lead us to take this kind of action at times, but this isn't a given in every situation.

Too often, we are tempted to fear a broad range of people. Many people experience an existential dread of anyone who doesn't look and think like themselves—or whom they simply don't know—believing they intend to cause harm. Many people believe someone out there desires to take what's theirs and ruin their way of life.

We are wrong to think that people of a different class, language, nationality, religion, political party, etc. are less trustworthy than others solely due to these classifications. We sin when we judge whole groups of people as bad because of one or more of these differences. Either Jesus loves and died for everyone in the world, or he did not. Recall that Paul states, "There is neither Jew nor Gentile, neither slave nor free, nor is there male and female, for you are all one in Christ Jesus" (Gal 3:28).

For example, some people who have money judge those who don't. They may verbally acknowledge the exceptions—especially for anyone they know personally. Yet they will generalize all those in poverty as lazy and out to steal their money through government programs. On the flip side, many working class people will judge all those with more wealth as being greedy, evil, hoarding money for themselves while not paying workers enough.

Both extremes can claim an element of truth since there are people who fit these stereotypes. The problem is when we pre-judge everyone in a group. Using the above example, it's a gross oversimplification to believe that all wealthy people are greedy, or all poor people are lazy. Good and bad people exist in most groups. Fear isn't the only reason for being prejudiced against others, but fear of being taken advantage of and fear of there not being enough both play a role.

The following two chapters examine love specifically. But I quickly want to look at one applicable example of God's love. If we want to be consistent in saying that Jesus loves everyone, we must believe that he loved the Pharisees. Reading through the Gospels, it's easy to see the religious leaders as the enemy. Jesus certainly has some harsh words for them, but he didn't dehumanize them or wish their death. Quite the contrary—he desired their repentance and his actions were directed to that end.

Jesus commanded his disciples to go into all the world as representatives of his kingdom. Presumably as they did so, they would encounter people with different backgrounds, different cultures, different languages, and different ethnicities. Jesus didn't say to love these people only if they learned Hebrew or got circumcised or supported the "right" Roman emperor. Jesus didn't promote building walls around Israel to keep others out.

Instead, he taught that we should be like the Father, who causes rain to fall on both the righteous and unrighteous (Matt 5:45).

Fear and love are like oil and water. Fear of our neighbor causes us to protect ourselves at the cost of our neighbor. Jesus does the opposite. He serves humanity even at cost to himself.

How can we tell if we are responding to fear with prudence or sin? First, ask yourself if your fear is reasonable. Sometimes this questioning is all we need to recognize we are being unreasonable. However, we must be cautious knowing that our emotions can bias us to rationalize what we already feel. Am I simply attempting to protect myself against a nebulous, abstract, perceived threat, one that isn't truly grounded in reality?

Second, and perhaps most importantly, we need to ask how our response will affect others. Am I willing to even consider how my actions may affect others? Will my actions or the actions I am advocating for help others? Will they be inconsequential to others, or will they actually harm them? Am I effectively advocating to sacrifice the wellbeing of others in order to maintain my own sense of comfort? Or am I willing to consider others' points of view?

Below are examples of the contrast between fear and love.

Fear: Keep out the foreigner.

Love: Welcome the outsider. (Exod 23:9, Lev 19:33–34, Deut 10:18–19, Jer 22:3)

Fear: Avoid talking about sex (out of fear that this will lead to sexual sin).

Love: Teach about healthy sexuality. (Prov 22:6)

Fear: Condemn those who hold different views.

Love: Listen respectfully to those who hold different views.

Fear: Preach God's wrath and judgment out of fear that otherwise people will sin.

Love: Preach God's love and mercy so that people won't want to sin.

Fear: Exercise tight control over every group in the church because someone might say something doctrinally wrong.

Love: Allow others to exercise their own gifts and trust that God will take care of doctrine. (1 Cor 12:7, 13:26)

Fear: We mustn't dare question the institutions that supposedly protect us.

Love: When a person claims to have been hurt by an institution, we can consider their story.

Fear: Governments, politicians, and/or other groups are conspiring to ruin our way of life.

Love: Though there are corrupt people and institutions, many in leadership are doing their best for their constituents.

Fear: We must homeschool our kids and only let them participate in Christian groups or else they might be taught something contrary to our beliefs (a wall of sorts).

Love: We can allow our kids to attend schools and/or participate in groups that aren't specifically Christian, and we can guide them through whatever they encounter.

We, as ambassadors of Christ both individually and collectively, must learn to love others despite our fears. Jesus has given us this ability through his resurrection from the dead. Because of the resurrection, we can choose to risk ourselves instead of sacrificing the wellbeing of other people. God empowers us through the cross because we know that no matter what happens, God is more powerful.

When you find yourself anxious, worried, hesitant, or even angry (which can come from feeling threatened), ask yourself what you are really afraid of. Try to identify the issue behind the fear. For example, if a bear runs across my path, I could say I am afraid of the bear. But behind this, I'm afraid of being injured and subsequently having a major disruption to my life. After identifying your fear, consider what this fear is urging you to do. Ask if this is a godly or worldly response.

Your fears may be preventing you from living the full life that God desires for you. As you study scripture and pray, ask God to reveal your unreasonable fears. Ask him to give you the courage to take the steps he wants despite your fears. Facing our fears is one aspect of the journey to healthy Christianity. And we can use our fear of missing God's desire for our lives to fight our natural, fleshly reactions to our other fears.

I hope that you will hold your fear in check while reading the remainder of this book. Some ideas may at first seem scary. However, I want this book to help guide you to a more resilient faith. A dead, brittle tree will break in the wind. A healthy tree, however, is flexible enough to bend but not break.

* * *

Fear is a vital human emotion. However, because of our fallen nature, our fear may urge us to act in a way that is contrary to Christ's love. As it is written, "In your anger, do not sin" (Eph 4:26), so also we must avoid sinning out of our fear.

Love Is a Verb

"Dear children, let us not love with words or speech but with actions and in truth." 1 John 3:18

"This is how we know what love is: Jesus Christ laid down his life for us. And we ought to lay down our lives for our brothers and sisters." 1 John 3:16

Love is the most important concept in Christianity. To this day, Jews recite the Shema: *Hear oh Israel, the Lord our God, the Lord is one. Love the Lord your God with all your heart, mind, and soul* (Deut 6:4–5). Jesus stated that this is the most important commandment, along with its partner: "Love your neighbor as yourself" (Mark 12:28–31, Matt 22:35–40).

Many Christians, surprisingly, seem uncomfortable with the idea of God's love. They often feel compelled to tag on "and just" or "and truth" or make another counterbalance. However, John doesn't say that God is love *and* (fill in the blank). He says, "God is love" (1 John 4:8, 16). That statement ends with a period. So I can only imagine that some Christians misunderstand the meaning of love.

In his book *The Four Loves*, C. S. Lewis made famous the multiple words in Greek[1] all translated into our single English word *love*. Even without knowing Greek, it should be obvious that we use the term *love* in a broad variety of ways. I certainly hope you don't love your spouse the same way you love a pumpkin spiced latte, for example. If you do, you're probably in for a rocky marriage!

In our culture, often the first thing the word *love* brings to mind is the "romantic" type of desire. This type of love leads with emotion. The corresponding work in Greek is *eros*, the root of our English word *erotic*. So, yes, this type of love also relates to sexual desire and attraction.

It seems difficult to find a movie or song that doesn't have something to do with the "romantic" type of love. We even have a holiday dedicated to it—Valentine's Day. Countless books have been written about love, sex, and relationships. People have high hopes for love (though too frequently our experiences don't live up to our dreams).

If we believe that Jesus was fully human as the Bible depicts, then he quite likely experienced this erotic type of desire. "Falling in love" and having sexual desire is a normal part of how God made us. It's what we choose to do with our desires which can be good or bad. And though he would have experienced these feelings, Jesus, of course, did not sin in how he dealt with them (Heb 4:15).

We can also think about the way we love our family and friends. "Romantic" love can be incredibly strong, but it's difficult to beat the love parents have for their children. Little doubt this is why the Bible reveals God as a father. We may also have a friend who is as close if not closer than a sibling. We love them and vice versa. Our bond with them can be very strong as well.

While it hopefully goes beyond this, when we talk about our love for our family and friends, the first thing many of us have in mind is our *feelings* toward them.

In a similar vein, we talk about how we love pizza, the Bahamas, the Chicago Cubs, horses, Taylor Swift, chocolate, *Star Wars*, Starbucks coffee, Graeter's ice cream, Chick-fil-A, etc. Unless you're one of the few people who knows Taylor personally, these are all objects. We say we love things when we really like them, when they bring us pleasure.

The varieties of love we have talked about so far share one thing in common: they mostly describe how we *feel* about the object of our love. These feelings are good, not bad. But when we talk about God's love, we're talking about something very different.

When the Bible says that God is love, it's not saying that God is a big bag of sappy feelings. Neither does it mean that God is a pushover, like a sweet grandparent who can't say no. God expresses aspects of love for us similar to how we love our closest family and friends. But this isn't the type of love that John used when he defined God as love.

Instead, John uses the Greek word *agape* to describe the way God loves. This type of love is more an action than a feeling. "Love is a verb," as D.C. Talk sang.

> Love is patient, love is kind. It does not envy, it does not boast, it is not proud. It does not dishonor others, it is not self-seeking, it is not easily angered, it keeps no record of wrongs. Love does not delight in evil but rejoices with the truth. It always protects, always trusts, always hopes, always perseveres. (1 Cor 13:4–7)

Paul describes actions or concepts expressed through action. My favorite definition of this type of love is that *love is seeking what is best for the other*. This boils it down to the core of love. I've also heard it said that, "Love is doing what you don't want to do because you want to." Love certainly doesn't always have to be difficult or taking unwanted action. However, love does what is best for the other even when one does not feel like doing it at that moment.

That said, this type of love isn't dispassionate. Instead, it is so deep that it persists regardless of the response of the person receiving the love, and this love is willing to sacrifice oneself for the other. It goes beyond a mere "strong like" for the person.

> Who shall separate us from the love of Christ? Shall trouble or hardship or persecution or famine or nakedness or danger or sword? . . . No, in all these things we are more than conquerors through him who loved us. For I am convinced that neither death nor life, neither angels nor demons, neither the present nor the future, nor any powers, neither height nor depth, nor anything else in all creation, will be able to separate us from the love of God that is in Christ Jesus our Lord (Rom 8:35, 37–39).

> God demonstrates his own love for us in this: While we were still sinners, Christ died for us (Rom 5:8).

Soon after the prior verse, Paul addresses one of the big fears that keep many Christians from fully embracing God's love. They fear that if we fully accept God's love, people will feel they have a pass to sin. But Paul counters this. "Shall we go on sinning so that grace may increase? By no means! We are those who have died to sin; how can we live in it any longer?" (Rom 6:1–2).

God, as a perfect and loving father, deeply desires the best for us. Love (*agape*) doesn't just mean he gives us everything we want. Just as a parent often knows better than a child what is good for the child, God knows what will be best for us and seeks to bring this into our lives.[2] He can be firm, but never out of anger at us; rather, he acts out of true love for us.

When John tells us that God is love, it is this *agape* type of love that he is communicating. He wants us to know that God seeks the best for each person as well as creation as a whole. "We know that in all things God works for the good of those who love him" (Rom 8:28).

Love requires more than one person. God has the ability to define love within himself because of the three persons of the trinity. The Father, Son, and Spirit perfectly express *agape* love toward one another. God is love because God is triune.

God's posture toward us is *love*, before we even do anything—even before we believed in him or Jesus. As we saw, he loved us while we were still sinners. "Therefore, let us approach the throne of grace with confidence" (Heb 4:16). We can petition God with confidence because we know we are his children and that he loves us (1 John 3:1).

To build on the first chapter, we mustn't let fear keep us from experiencing God's love or keep us from loving others.

In the next chapter, we'll more fully explore God's love.

* * *

The word *love* is used to describe a broad range of feelings and behaviors. God's love is much more than just sappy feelings. God's love acts for the good of the other even at cost to himself.

Who Do You Say That I Am?

———— • ————

"See what great love the Father has lavished on us, that we should be called children of God! And that is what we are!" 1 John 3:1

"A new command I give you: Love one another. As I have loved you, so you must love one another. By this everyone will know that you are my disciples, if you love one another." John 13:34–35

"Let no debt remain outstanding, except the continuing debt to love one another, for whoever loves others has fulfilled the law. . . Love does no harm to a neighbor. Therefore love is the fulfillment of the law." Romans 13:8

In 1741, the Puritan Jonathan Edwards preached a famous sermon titled, "Sinners in the Hands of an Angry God" (a book I was required to read in school). He expresses the sentiment that God is ready to release anyone who doesn't follow Christ into the fiery torment of hell.

Edwards wasn't the first to express such a view of God, nor would he be the last. The great Reformer John Calvin famously emphasized God's sovereignty, which included the idea that God chose who he would send to hell. Calvin was trained in law and, along with other Reformed theologians, expressed the "penal substitutionary" view of Jesus's atonement. This paradigm views Christ's death in legal terms. People's sins violated God's law and God subsequently demands death for these violations. While we deserve this punishment, Jesus takes this on our behalf, thus shielding us from God's wrath.

Let me paraphrase a common view of God and ourselves (a.k.a. theology), one similar to what many Christians hold: God is perfect and holy, so much so that no imperfect being can exist in his presence. God created humanity. But because of sin, we're now "totally depraved," meaning there is no good in us whatsoever. We are completely incapable of good and, left to our own devices, will do nothing but evil thanks to being born with sin. God—perfect and holy as he is—can't even look at us. This is why God the Father turned away from Jesus on the cross. All of this sin must be punished and atoned for in order to achieve justice. We deserve nothing but death. However, God in his love decided to send Jesus to die in our place. Now, when we get to heaven, God will let us in because he won't actually see us but will only see Jesus instead!

The above may not capture the nuances that the original theologians held, but it's a good summary of how it has filtered down to many lay people.

Let's look at an actual statement made by the Gospel Coalition in which they define the gospel as follows:

> The Bible depicts human beings, all human beings everywhere, as in revolt against God, and therefore under his judgment. But although God stands over against us in judgment because of our sin, quite amazingly he stands over against us in love, because he is that kind of God—and the gospel is the good news of what God, in love, has done in Jesus Christ, especially in Jesus's cross and resurrection, to deal with our sin and to reconcile us to himself.

> Christ bore our sin on the cross. He bore the penalty, turned aside God's judgment, God's wrath, from us, and cancelled sin. The brokenness of our lives he restores; the shattered relationships he rebuilds in the

> context of the church; the new life that we human beings find in Christ is granted out of the sheer grace of God. It is received by faith as we repent of our sins and turn to Jesus. We confess him as Lord, and bow to him joyfully.[3]

Many Christians would more or less agree with the descriptions of God above. But many have a jumbled view of God, demonstrated in the GC's description of the gospel above.

> But although God stands over against us in judgment because of our sin, quite amazingly he stands over against us in love, because he is that kind of God . . . The sheer grace of God . . . turned aside God's judgment, God's wrath.

God judges us . . . because he loves us? His grace turned away his wrath, but only because he let it out by torturing his son to death? Does this really make sense? If, due to sin, we are completely evil, why does God still love us? Are we saying God loves evil? If, due to sin, we're nothing more than excrement, why does God still love us? Are we saying God loves poop? How does Jesus's death make up for our sin? How is it that God feels all of this wrath toward us but also loves us? Does God really love us if he only accepts us when we are "covered" by Jesus or, in other words, when he only sees Jesus? If this is the case, does God really love us?

I find it interesting which characteristics many Christians emphasize about God versus those God likes to emphasize about himself. When Christians talk about God now days, they often talk about the "omnis": omniscient (all knowing), omni-present (present everywhere at once), omnipotent (all powerful). Yet it is interesting that when God reveals himself to Moses in the Bible, the first qualities he highlights are his *compassion and mercy.*

> The Lord, the Lord, the compassionate and gracious God, slow to anger, abounding in love and faithfulness, maintaining love to thousands, and forgiving wickedness, rebellion and sin (Exod 34:6–7).

Of course Jesus further emphasized these characteristics of God when he began his ministry. If God chooses to emphasize his compassion, why do many Christian want to emphasize his holiness and "otherness"? Yes, God is so far beyond us as to be incomprehensible in his entirety. Yet certain theologies take this to an extreme. A number of God's attributes comprise part of his character. Emphasizing one (such as God's sovereignty) to the point at which it trumps all the others creates a distorted, grotesque image of our creator.

God created humanity along with the rest of creation and declared his creation to be good. In fact, after he creates people, he states that the creation is *very good* (Gen 1:31). Yes, we did sin and continue to sin now. But does that entirely vaporize every bit of goodness we were created with? No. God doesn't love us *as* dung; God loves us *despite* our dung.

Some preachers seem to almost have fun describing how terribly worthless we are. Many Christians soak this up as well. While this may fit their theology, it is difficult to reconcile with real world experience. Many people do not claim to follow Christ, yet they are kind, caring, peaceful, and even make sacrifices for others.

Those teaching total depravity find inspiration in Romans 3, where Paul quotes from several passages in the Old Testament:

"There is no one righteous, not even one; there is no one who understands; there is no one who seeks God. All have turned away, they have together become worthless; there is no one who does good,   not even one." "Their throats are open graves; their tongues practice deceit." "The poison of vipers is on their lips." "Their mouths are full of cursing and bitterness." "Their feet are swift to shed blood;   ruin and misery mark their ways, and the way of peace they do not know." "There is no fear of God before their eyes." (3:10–18)

This does paint a bleak picture of humanity. But Paul wants to convey the point that no one is completely righteous in and of themselves. No man is good enough to justify himself. No woman is holy and perfect enough to save herself. But acknowledging our sinfulness does not mean that no one can do *anything* good on their own.

The reality is, we are a mixed bag. We all do good and we all do bad. It's not difficult to look around the world today or in the past and recognize that people have an incredible capacity to commit unbelievably heinous and evil acts. On the extreme end, people commit genocide, torture, murder, rape, and other ways of denying others' humanity. However, we see countless examples of people who love others, give to the needy, feed the hungry, care for the sick, and even give their whole lives to the cause of helping people. Humans have done incredible acts of goodness. This isn't to say that everyone does an equal amount of good and bad. Yet no "good" person is entirely good, and no bad person is entirely bad.

* * *

Growing up, I heard that sin separates us from God. This is true to an extent, but not in the way people usually understand. The separation doesn't come from God's side. This misunderstanding comes primarily from one passage in Habakkuk:

You are of purer eyes than to behold
evil, and cannot look on wickedness (1:13
NKJV).

It's important to note that *this is a statement
Habakkuk is making to God, not a truth God is claiming for
himself.* Second, in the context, this statement is poetic,
part of praising the goodness of God. If we consider this
logically, we would sound silly to claim God literally
can't see the wrong that people do. It's obvious that God
is aware of wrong, else he could not bring about future
justice.

In the New Testament, Jesus claims to be the image
of God, so much so that when Philip asks, "Show us the
Father," Jesus responds with, "Here I am!" (John 14:8–9).
It's clear in the Gospels that when Jesus encounters a
sinner, he never responds with, "Argh! I'm too holy!
I'm melting!" Nor does any "sinner" spontaneously
combust in Jesus's presence. Instead, Jesus earned a
reputation for hanging out with sinners. So either God
can be in the presence of and see people despite their sin,
or Jesus is not God.

The idea is also supported by a misunderstanding
of Jesus's cry, "My God, my God, why have you forsaken
me?" The common interpretation of his cry says that
God, being so holy, must turn up his nose and can't
possibly be tainted by seeing Jesus—*God's own son whom*

he sent for this purpose—because Jesus was somehow polluted by sin.

This understanding is a massive failure in theology on Christians' part. Yes, the Bible emphasizes God's holiness. But in his holiness, God pursues humanity and emphasizes his love, compassion, and mercy. God isn't a stuck-up, spoiled person who refuses to be tainted by anything or anyone deemed to be below him—which would be everything. Instead, he continually shows up despite our mess, offering to guide us in a better way.

This belief about God turning his back on his son is also a massive failure on Christians' part to understand *poetry*. Emotions. Feelings. We all have them. They defy logic and reason. Emotions don't define reality, but they are a part of our reality. *"Why have you forsaken me?"* Do you believe that Jesus, while being crucified, was logically, in an abstract manner, philosophizing about God and choosing to make a theological statement at this point in time? I doubt it! Was God the Father forsaking Jesus? *It sure as heck felt like it, no doubt!*

It's insightful that Jesus's mind, at this worst moment, turned to scripture to express his torment. When Jews cited scripture, they often quoted the first verse to invoke a whole passage. Jesus quotes the beginning of Psalm 22. Yet if one continues reading they will come to,

For he has not despised or scorned   the suffering of the afflicted one; he has not hidden his face from him but has listened to his cry for help.

Did God the Father abandon Jesus on the cross due to the sin he bore? Psalm 22 says that, despite it appearing that way, God "has not hidden his face from him but has listened to his cry for help."

The degree to which we are cut off from God the Father is only on our part—not God's. Jesus *felt* forsaken *because sin was what brought about his crucifixion.* In reality, God the Father loved Jesus every bit as much at this point as at any other. Similarly, our sin may cause us to feel shame and self-loathing and subsequently far from God. But again, those feelings don't mean God has forsaken us.

The mistaken understanding that God might forsake me affected me early in my faith journey. I thought my salvation might be in question if I were to die after sinning but before confessing and asking God for forgiveness. Again, this doesn't align with the basis of our salvation. My salvation isn't based on my "works" or merit; it's based on God's grace and mercy through Jesus's death and resurrection. We do not vacillate between in and out, saved and damned, by every little action we take or feeling we have.

A passage that worries many sincere Christians is found in the Sermon on the Mount. In Matthew 7, Jesus says,

> Not everyone who says to me, "Lord, Lord," will enter the kingdom of heaven, but only the one who does the will of my

Father who is in heaven. Many will say
to me on that day, "Lord, Lord, did we
not prophesy in your name and in your
name drive out demons and in your name
perform many miracles?" Then I will tell
them plainly, "I never knew you. Away
from me, you evildoers!" (vv 21–23)

It's understandable why this concerns people. Take
the first part: a person prophesies and performs miracles
in Jesus's name. Without any additional context, it
would sound like the person described is a sincere,
devout, fully committed follower of Jesus, likely even
a missionary or other vocational minister. If Jesus can
deny knowing this person and call them an evildoer,
how can anyone be confident that they actually follow
Christ?

Does Jesus want or expect his follows to doubt their
status? Does he want even the most devout to worry
about their salvation and live in fear of potentially being
sent to hell? This doesn't seem right. What is going on
here?

When you encounter a passage that is confusing on
its own such as this, step back to look at the broader
context. Prior to this passage under examination, Jesus
warns against false prophets. He teaches that one can
discern true and false prophets by the "fruit" (results)
of their work. Jesus then talks about how he will deny
some who claim to be working in his name. After this, he

provides the analogy of a person who built their house on sand versus one who built on rock. He says this to encourage his listeners to put his teachings into action as opposed to only listening to them.

The point here, in context, seems to be that some people who use the name of Jesus won't actually do what he taught. These people shouldn't expect to be saved. But the teaching is less for these people; Jesus warns those who were in danger of being fooled by those people. In other words, don't believe and follow any and every person who claims to be teaching the ways of Christ. Rather, we should discern their authenticity by how well they follow the teachings of Jesus themselves and based on if their teaching is bringing forth good or bad "fruit."

If we are sincerely living the type of life Jesus would live—not that we are perfect—would a good and loving Father want us to live constantly terrified that we may end up in hell? No! It doesn't seem to be in character for a parent to want their child to live in a state of terror. After all, "perfect love drives out fear, because fear has to do with punishment" (1 John 4:18). Furthermore,

> Who shall separate us from the love of Christ? Shall trouble or hardship or persecution or famine or nakedness or danger or sword? . . . I am convinced that neither death nor life, neither angels nor demons, neither the present nor the

future, nor any powers, neither height nor
depth, nor anything else in all creation,
will be able to separate us from the love of
God that is in Christ Jesus our Lord (Rom
8:35, 38–39).

All this isn't to say, "Once saved, always saved."
But our salvation isn't so fragile as to be put into
doubt by any little misstep on our part. God's love
is bigger than our doubts and doesn't require perfect
theology. As quoted from John above, love and the fear of
punishment are opposed; God loves us and doesn't want
us—his children—to live in fear of punishment.

* * *

Humility is a virtue. Pride is a sin. However, humility
isn't thinking lowly of oneself. Instead, humility means
thinking *accurately* about oneself. The Bible tells us that
we are "fearfully and wonderfully made" (Ps 139:14).
As mentioned previously, when God finishes creating
humankind, he declared his creation to be *very good* (Gen
1:31). It's worth restating: *we were created very good in
God's image.*

Scripture instructs us to "love one another as you
love yourself" (Lev 19:18). If you believe you are a
worthless pile of garbage, how well will you treat
yourself, *a person whom God loves?* And if you believe you

are worthless, isn't that attitude likely to affect how well you can "love others as yourself"?

Throughout his ministry, Jesus clearly demonstrates how God loves people. Jesus's command isn't to think terribly of oneself. Instead, he calls on us to love others just as he demonstrated love to us.

Scripture also instructs us not to judge others. What does this mean? There has been a fair amount of confusion regarding judgment, especially since Paul also says that we *should* be able to judge (1 Cor 6:1–6). When we're instructed not to judge, it means that we're not to *condemn* others.

One of the most critical ideas to understand is that we must not divide people into "rankings." To condemn a person is to believe that a person *deserves* to be mistreated, disrespected, or to otherwise be on the receiving end of something bad. On the flip side, we might also judge a person as deserving of better, more preferential treatment than others. In other words, judging creates a scale for people in which we consider some worthy of receiving more honor and respect and others worthy of receiving disrespect and dishonor.

We are no better than or worse than anyone in terms of our humanity, just differently gifted. Some people are especially intelligent or gifted in art, for example. Others possess great athletic talent. It's not wrong to acknowledge this or to be proud of one's achievements. It only becomes wrong if a person subsequently believes their talent makes them innately more *worthy* than others.

Note that judgment (condemnation) differs from discernment. Discernment comes from wisdom. Say for example one has been in an abusive relationship. Recognizing that one should abandon an abusive relationship shows discernment. Discernment carries no ill will. In contrast, judgment would condemn the abuser as innately evil and as someone who therefore deserves to be hit by a bus.[4]

Though no one may say this or think this consciously, many people think of others as either entirely good or bad. We often recognize a good action and subsequently label that person as "good". Similarly, people frequently label someone as "bad" when they learn of something bad that the person has done (or is rumored to have done). This oversimplification demonstrates black-and-white or binary thinking.

One problematic result is that people may deny that a "good" person could do any wrong, even despite evidence and/or allegations to the contrary. For example, oftentimes pastors have been protected and defended against alleged abuse for this reason. On the other side, if someone is labeled "bad," then people believe they deserve mistreatment—or even death. Furthermore, these people may believe that even they themselves are justified in carrying out these punishments. But God does not take such a posture toward us.

Jesus refers to God as his Father. We know God is good, perfect, and loving. He isn't a temperamental hothead, just ready to blow up at any little infraction that offends him. God loves us and wants the best for us. He is not a pagan god who demands sacrifices in order to appease his wrath.

God's posture toward us is *love*, before we even do anything—even before we believed in him or Jesus. He loved us while we were still sinners (Rom 5:8). This is again in contrast to pagan Gods who are angry and demanding.

"Therefore, let us approach the throne of grace with confidence" (Heb 4:16). We can petition God with confidence because we know we are his children and that he loves us (1 John 3:1).

Some Christians have taught that, when we sin, we break God's heart. This belief has elicited deep concern among some believers, and understandably so. Of course we want to please God and not to do anything that breaks his heart. But we ought not feel that we deeply grieve God by every minor imperfection in our lives.

If God is a perfect father, then he will grieve when we engage in behaviors that harm ourselves and others. Yet God does not emotionally manipulate us. It's especially important to know that God is not disappointed in us as a whole, nor does he think we are failures. If God truly loves us unconditionally as he says he does, this means he loves us even if we never do a single thing for him!

This, of course, does not mean we won't respond to his love, as James makes clear (see 2:14–26). However, we can be free of the burden of feeling as though his feelings toward us are dependent on us.

We experience godly conviction when we realize we need to do something different. But godly conviction brings no sense of shame or self-loathing. It does not make us think we are terrible people. How can we hate ourselves if God loves us so much? No, self-hatred is of the devil.

Our understanding of God's love influences our understanding of faith and prayer. Some Christians believe that answers to prayers are solely a matter of faith. Certainly, the Bible talks about the importance of faith in prayer. "The prayer of a righteous person is powerful and effective" (Jas 5:16). Yet a lot more is involved in determining whether a petition to God is fulfilled as requested. Why do I bring this up?

For Christians who believe prayer relies solely on one's faith, an unanswered prayer can only mean a lack of faith. This has definitely been used to kick people at their lowest moments. Naturally, people's most fervent prayers occur during the worse times of their lives. To tell them that God hasn't answered their prayers because they don't have enough faith is a gut-punch that knocks the wind out of God's child.

When we experience terrible events out of our control, such as a terminal illness or collapse of a marriage, God does not sit around waiting for us to pray with enough faith. He is not testing us or teaching us a lesson (even if we may learn something through it). Instead, God grieves with us. Explaining why these kind of things happen and why God doesn't step in and heal in an instant is beyond the scope of this chapter. But understand, God is with you through hard times. While he didn't cause these things to happen, he is always working to bring the best out of difficult circumstances.

* * *

God's unqualified love is foundational. We can and should have confidence in his love for us. This love frees us from fear and allows us to love others.

It's All In Your Head!

―――――――― • ――――――――

"I am sending you out like sheep among wolves. Therefore be as shrewd as snakes and as innocent as doves." Matthew 10:16

"It is true that some preach Christ out of envy and rivalry... not sincerely." Philippians 1:15, 17

The field of psychology is surprisingly new in the history of the world. It only began to develop in the early twentieth century (though origins were laid in the mid-nineteenth), later than the development of evangelicalism, which arose after the U.S. Civil War, and potentially took place within the lifetime of our parents or grandparents. Early psychology held many odd ideas which have since been superseded. But the early breakthrough was in recognizing how feelings, beliefs, and desires motivate us unconsciously or semiconsciously. Prior to this, people believed we made most decisions rationally.

Christianity involves beliefs and practices, but it just as often involves emotions and spirituality as well. These overlap with the fields of mental and emotional health to a large degree. Some Christians balk at the idea of psychology because they wish to hold to a belief that every problem (at least those non-physical) can be fixed solely with spiritual solutions. Some will maintain that a person just needs enough faith and prayer and God will resolve any malady one is experiencing.

God can certainly step in and heal people, and many have experienced such healing. More often than not, however, God uses the seemingly mundane means of working through other people. If a believer is diagnosed with cancer, we pray for them and rightly so. Nevertheless, most Christians still believe that the person should follow the care and treatments of physicians. Prayer, faith, and practical—even "secular" care—are not at odds. However, more Christians have been suspicious when it comes to the field of mental health. I believe this is partially due to the odd ideas of early psychology, especially those related to sexuality.

Fortunately, younger people are more informed about and comfortable with discussing mental health. Nevertheless, since psychology is a newer discipline, and due to Christianity's rocky start with it, certain common aspects of Christianity at times have led to poorer mental wellbeing.

* * *

Before I discuss factors that lead to poorer mental, emotional, and spiritual health, I want to describe what health looks like in these areas. Unfortunately, many of us grew up without understanding exactly what it looks like to be healthy in these ways. Because of this, unhealthy practices can seem quite normal.

Mental, emotional, and spiritual health are so closely related in my mind that it's difficult to separate them. The mental health field largely deals with how people feel. Psychology studies human behavior, specifically the motivations for why we do the things we do. Our thoughts—our intellect—plays a part in this, but much of what drives us are our feelings and desires, many of which we may not even be aware of.

The American Psychological Association defines mental health as:

> A state of mind characterized by emotional well-being, good behavioral adjustment, relative freedom from anxiety and disabling symptoms, and a capacity to establish constructive relationships and cope with the ordinary demands and stresses of life.[5]

Self-esteem is one important aspect of mental wellness. We should believe we are deserving of health, relationships, respect, and well-being. We should also believe we are neither uniquely bad and worthless, nor uniquely worthy of extraordinary preferential treatment. In other words, we are mentally healthy when we have a reasonable and moderate self-conception. It is unhealthy to think we are more important than we are or less important than we are.

When we are mentally healthy, we also understand boundaries. We know that each person is responsible for their own emotions and actions. We are neither too aggressive nor too passive. We believe we have people in our life who love and support us. We can express our needs and desires without needing to be ashamed. We understand we can share our thoughts and feelings with "safe" people, and that we won't be met with derision. We also know that not every person is safe and are generally able to discern the appropriate amount to share based on the level of closeness and safety in a relationship. We recognize unhealthy relationships and avoid and/or put boundaries up with these people. We understand we are responsible for our own actions and are able to make decisions and take action. We realize we don't have to be perfect in order to continue to receive love.

When we are emotionally healthy, we experience a normal range of emotions: happiness, sadness, fear, anger, etc. We are aware of our emotions and respond to them in an appropriate way. That said, emotions are often subtle, so we won't always be perfect in recognizing and responding to them. Nevertheless, an emotionally healthy person will generally be able to avoid the worst responses. For example, hitting your spouse is a bad way of responding to anger. Saying everything is fine while giving them the cold shoulder is also an unhealthy way to deal with anger. In contrast, simply telling your spouse that you feel angry with them is an emotionally healthy way to handle your anger. We call this ability emotional intelligence.

Everyone has experiences that challenge their emotional wellbeing. We have to put a certain amount of effort into maintaining emotional health just as we do physical and spiritual health. But beyond this, some people will experience certain mental or emotional illnesses not common to all. Similar to physical conditions, these can range from mild and temporary to debilitating and incurable. Some mental illnesses happen through no one's fault. A person can experience a mental disorder that arises naturally due to the close link between our bodies and mind. On the other hand, some mental and emotional problems do arise due to actions taken by others.

Discussing all types of mental disorders is way beyond the scope of this book. What I do want to examine in the remainder of the chapter is what a mentally and emotionally healthy Christian looks like and how to avoid actions leading to unhealthiness in these areas.

* * *

Our immediate family is the first community most of us experience. Ideally, one's family functions as a healthy, supportive group. Parents should love their children by providing for them, teaching them to become fully functioning adults, encouraging them, valuing and supporting them, setting up boundaries and disciplining as appropriate, and showing them love and affection.

Adult family members should respect one another as equals. They should support and encourage one another and communicate clearly and honestly. They shouldn't be dishonest, saying something doesn't matter when it clearly does, for example. Nor should they attempt to manipulate others in the family through their words or actions. Decisions affecting the family should be made through mutual negotiation in contrast to one person dictating. Families should be with us through the ups and downs that invariably happen in life. We ought to be accepted at both our best and our worst.

I describe family here because of the comparison the Bible makes to the body of Christ.

> Who are my mother and my brothers?"
> [Jesus] asked. Then he looked at those
> seated in a circle around him and said,
> "Here are my mother and my brothers!

Whoever does God's will is my brother
and sister and mother (Mark 3:34–35).[6]

In the New Testament, Jesus's followers are often referred to as brothers and sisters. More than just a cute metaphor, the community of Christ-followers is intended to act similarly to a family in certain respects. Jesus wants us to support one another, to encourage each other, and to work together to do his will in the world as much as possible. We're constantly told to encourage and strengthen one another. Each member should have the best interest of others in mind.

Unfortunately, like our biological families, communities of Christ followers aren't perfect. It is spiritually unhealthy when one member of the body tries to force another member to conform to their own understanding of Christianity. Some Christians hold convictions about how they think every "true" follower of Christ should think, what they should believe, what they should say, how they should act, and how they should feel, both right now and at all times. Following Christ is important, and the desire for others to do the same is understandable, but sometimes Christians try to force everyone else to fall in line. However, Jesus doesn't force us to follow him, and we shouldn't try to pressure others to either. Though we may desire that people we know will follow Christ, we must remember that he desires this even more than we do. And he wants us to do this voluntarily.

The Spirit gives each believer different spiritual gifts. Some Christians have a greater gift of faith than others. These believers can have an unwavering confidence in God. Not all of us have this gift as abundantly as others. For many, our spiritual journey goes through ups and downs, highs and lows. We talk about mountaintop experiences. On the flip side, the so-called "dark night of the soul" is a common experience among faithful followers of Christ as well. The one with more faith should use their faith to encourage fellow believers, not to demand that other Christ-followers express the same level of faith that they themselves possess.

We should want the best for each other and do what we can to support each other in our spiritual journeys. We can teach and encourage our fellow brothers and sisters, but we should understand that each person's spiritual life is a journey. As such, we shouldn't try to force them to be in the same spot in their journey as we are in ours, nor to possess the same gifts.

* * *

As Christians, we believe that God has given us guidance on how to live. Some of that guidance comes in the form of general wisdom, while other aspects of God's teaching resemble specific universal rules. Christians may debate which of these categories a value falls under, but we agree on the existence of morality—"right" and "wrong" behavior.

Christians feel a significant need to convince people, especially those who claim to follow Jesus, of these beliefs and to follow this morality. Protestant theology holds that salvation comes to us via grace and not works (our actions). Nevertheless, many Christians in practice seem somewhat confused on this point. In fairness, the book of James makes it clear that if we have been saved, our behaviors will be transformed (though this sanctification is often a slow process; see 2:14–26). At the time the Bible was written, people understood belief and action as identical—to believe was to act accordingly.

Though it may not be theologically accurate to say that sin bars one from salvation, Christians often still feel that our actions have eternal life and death consequences. With the stakes so high, it's understandable why Christians feel so much pressure to get everyone to believe and behave.

We know that fear motivates. We feel so strongly about our beliefs that we sometimes slide into coercion to convince others to stay within the "lines" of orthodoxy (right belief) and orthopraxy (right behavior).

The temptation to use coercion is further exacerbated by the fact that many people, by personality, feel significant anxiety when they don't perceive the society in which they live as orderly and traditional. These people are likely to be religious as well since Christianity is a long existing tradition. So a significant impulse exists within religion to maintain control and order. Many Christians deeply fear lurking chaos that they sense at their doorstep.

This brings us full circle back to the beginning of the book when we talked about fear. As explained in chapter 1, fear can be helpful and unhelpful. Paul says, "In your anger, do not sin" (Ps 4:4 as quoted in Eph 4:26). Anger isn't a sin, but we can react to anger in a sinful way. Similarly, fear isn't a sin, but we can react to fear in a sinful way.

We shouldn't attempt to manipulate others due to our fear, even if we are trying to get them to act rightly. We may legitimately fear for their salvation. Nevertheless, God doesn't coerce us into following him. He has given us free will. It is clear that he wants us to choose to follow him. And we must remember that God desires others' salvation even more than we do.

We are to imitate Christ. If we behave in a way that attempts to manipulate others into following God, then we are not living like Jesus, no matter how well intentioned.

* * *

Unfortunately, some Christian leaders, churches, and/or organizations behave in ways which are mentally or emotionally unhealthy for their members. Such behavior can be tricky to recognize because it's not black and white. It's not that one church is 100 percent good while another church is 100 percent bad. God can and does work through all kinds of people and situations. God can bring healing and transformation to people's lives even if they attend a significantly unhealthy church.

God is strong enough to work through broken systems. Yet using God's work to justify or ignore problems with a leader or organization is a mistake. One warning sign to watch out for is when a leader, church, or organization is too enamored with themselves. They may talk about Jesus, God, and his kingdom, but in practice, they are building their own kingdom. They frequently talk about their own greatness and how others need to be a part of their church or ministry specifically. In other words, it's not just that they think people need to follow Jesus; they consider other Christians, churches, and ministries as deficient. This leader and/or church is unlikely to consider working with other ministries unless they are clearly in charge. A church or ministry like this may cite the number of conversions or baptisms they've seen. They hold that evidence of God's work must indicate the goodness of the church or ministry.

The attitude described above demonstrates the sin of pride and lack of humility. But a leader or church can go beyond this. A leader or church can believe God has specially chosen them. Now, this may actually be true to an extent. Perhaps God did want the pastor to be a Christian leader. Problems arise, however, when this person or organization believes they can't be questioned. Now, they likely never say this, but in practice, they message will be made clear that the leader is right and questions or disagreements put one at odds, not just with the leader, but with God.

Hopefully you can see the danger here. It's tricky, because God does want us to be his ambassadors in the world. So we should and do represent God. The problem comes when a leader consciously or unconsciously so closely aligns themselves with God that they believe they are effectively incapable of error.

Not only can a leader and/or organization begin to think they are more important than they are, but they can build a fortress of sorts in which they become unaccountable and unquestionable. Anyone who does question or disagree will be pushed down if not out entirely.

Every group of a certain number of people includes those who disagree. Just because one disagrees with a decision doesn't mean that this person is being ignored or mistreated. But I have heard stories in which even groups of elders have brought forward serious concerns only to be totally rebuffed. In an unhealthy system, anyone who is not the leader is immediately considered to be wrong. Watch out for organizations that lack real dialogue and where everyone who doesn't toe the line is ostracized.

The consequences of a disagreement are more severe than the initial point of contention in unhealthy churches. Sometimes, even the slightest perception of doubt in a person's loyalty can bring an inquisition. If a participant in a ministry (such as playing in a worship band or leading a small group) expresses doubts or concerns, they may be threatened that this "privilege" will be taken away if they don't get back in line. Or in worse cases, a person may be told to leave the church entirely. Since these organizations can consume a large part of someone's life, this may mean being cut off from one's entire social system. In fact, due to how they are enamored with themselves, unhealthy leaders will push people to become almost exclusively involved in the organization, minimizing one's connections outside of the group. Some churches or denominations even bar their members from communication with family members who've left the church.

Because the leader or ministry is seen as the manifestation of God on Earth *alone* (as opposed to in conjunction with the rest of the body of Christ), they require unwavering loyalty and dedication.

Toxic leaders can be given to a martyrdom complex as a way of deflecting even legitimate questions and disagreements. The leader can frame any lack of absolute support as being an example of evil at work to undermine their ministry. This strategy has the additional advantage of allowing the leader to frame themselves as the strong, powerful figure who stands for right in the face of resistance.

* * *

The term *spiritual abuse* has been coined for certain harmful behaviors that happen in religious institutions and/or by a religious authority. People who attend a church can commit other types of abuse: verbal, physical, psychological, etc. These don't necessarily constitute spiritual abuse. So what is spiritual abuse? Spiritual abuse happens when God, Christianity, and religious teaching are used to undermine a person's God-given autonomy and personhood. In other words, the abuse takes on a spiritual dimension when it is intertwined with God, the Bible, and Christianity. As a result, a person's spiritual life is harmed in addition to the other harms experienced.

For example, imagine a person brings a legitimate question or disagreement to a leader. If the pastor responds by slapping them in the face, he commits physical abuse. If the leader instead just berates and belittles them, he engages in verbal and psychological abuse. If, however, the pastor questions the person's faith, suggests they are going against God, and/or states that God feels displeased with the person because of their question or disagreement, he commits spiritual abuse. Why call it abuse? Because it inaccurately represents God in order to protect the leader and/or church by cutting down the accuser instead. It is spiritually abusive because it seems to shift the abuse off the leader and onto God.

Spiritual abuse should concern Christians because it communicates that God is actually the abuser. Spiritual abuse can easily destroy a person's faith. Now, you and I may be able to clearly differentiate and understand that abuse was just the result of a bad pastor or church and that this abuse does not invalidate Christianity. However, when Christianity is so closely intertwined with the abuse, victims often can't separate them. They may not be able to return to any church or faith, regardless of how good or right, without being emotionally triggered.

Spiritual abuse can be hard to discern for several reasons. If a pastor outright slaps someone in the face, clearly the pastor has transgressed. It is similar if the leader openly berates another person. In these instances, it is easier to recognize that a wrong has been done and the leader as the source of the bad behavior. Yet abuse often happens privately and the abuse frequently isn't as clear as the previous examples of physical and psychological abuse.

Because victims often see leaders as representing God, victims can associate any abuse by a Christian leader as tied to God. Thus when a person with some degree of spiritual authority commits an abuse, this abuse can have a significant spiritual element even if the abuser doesn't explicitly connect the abuse to God.

Pastors immersed in Christian teaching and Christian culture know how to use Christian language and the Bible to sound really holy, even if they say something untrue (intentionally or not). This can be difficult for church members to recognize without years of study.

Some Christians, including pastors, hold a theology that suggests we cannot do anything good on our own. We are wholly corrupt, they claim. They may teach people that every desire and impulse they have is bad. They may tell people they can't trust themselves but must instead only trust their religious leaders. I examined this theology in the chapter "Who Do You Say I Am?" but bring it up again here because it is important to understand how these beliefs impact our mental health.

Christians holding this kind of theology are taught not to trust themselves, to be deeply suspicious of their own thoughts and feelings, and to suppress their instincts and intuitions. This teaching may be done in attempt to control a congregation, in which case it constitutes spiritual abuse. But people can come to these conclusion themselves when involved in a church which emphasizes this theology.

God has given us intelligence, emotions, and intuitions. He has given us desires, instincts, and a conscience. God created us in his image and said we are good. It is true that we are fallen and that our own desires alone won't lead us to God's perfection.

However, this doesn't mean our senses are completely corrupt and evil. Far from it! Does a mother naturally love her child? Would we naturally react in anger if someone kicks a dog? Are we naturally thrilled to learn someone has been cured of cancer? It should be obvious that our heart and senses are not completely corrupted by our sinful nature.

We desire to eat and drink, good impulses that keep us alive. We may also desire to eat cake. This is where our intelligence should come into play. We can understand it is not good to eat cake every meal, so we can decide to take healthier actions. It's not that our desire for food is entirely bad, but we must realize that it isn't perfect on its own, either. We must discern the healthy course of action based on the wisdom God has given to us.

God has given us desires which, if enacted, will make the world a better place. For example, we may desire to have a family, which in part fulfills God's command to "Be fruitful and multiply" (Gen 1:28). Another example is that our instincts and intuitions can alert us when something is wrong. These intuitions are subtler but are nevertheless tools which God has given us to help us protect ourselves. God has given us instincts in part to keep us out of unhealthy relationships such as those described in this chapter.

Wisdom and discernment are crucial to determining when our desires urge us to something good (eating to live) or bad (eating only cake). God hasn't left us alone in this. First and foremost, he has given us his Spirit, who guides us and provides us with the godly wisdom we need. As Paul shared in Galatians,

> So I say, walk by the Spirit, and you will not gratify the desires of the flesh . . . The fruit of the Spirit is love, joy, peace, forbearance, kindness, goodness, faithfulness, gentleness and self-control (5:16, 22).

Spiritual abuse also happens when people use God and the Bible to keep people in abusive situations. The most common example is when wives are encouraged to stay with an abusive husband. Many a woman has been counseled that God wills her to remain in the marriage and be submissive in order that the husband "may be won over without words by the behavior of [his wife]" (1 Pet 3:1).

Yes, the above quote is scripture, but it is taken out of context and used to dismiss the legitimate concerns of women. Peter's instruction about winning over a husband relates to unbelievers—not marital abuse. In fact, if the goal were truly to "win over" an abusive husband, the better counsel would be for the victim to leave.

Staying in an abusive situation generally enables the abuse. After all, abuse requires a victim. Abusers often live in denial, unlikely to sense any need for change so long as the status quo remains. Many abusers will continue to deny they've acted in harmful ways. But they are even less likely to change so long as their spouse remains. No one gains by staying in abuse.

Neglect can also qualify as abuse. Let me speak specifically of those called to ministry. We often feel a sense of urgency and eternal importance to our mission. The great need means we always have something more to do. We may be tempted to think, "If I don't (fill in the blank), one more person might go hungry or might not find eternal salvation." However, we have forgotten that God intends us to work collectively. The salvation of the world (or just our community) does not rest on us alone. God cares about people more than we do, and he is plenty powerful enough to ensure that his will is accomplished.

Because of the great need and sense of calling, people in professional ministry can be tempted to become workaholics. Interestingly, I can't remember anyone talking about over work in the context of ministry. Because it is "the Lord's work," people may consider it laudable.

Professional clergy typically have families. When a clergy-person works non-stop, they give up significant time with their family. Ironically, it's tempting to end up "loving people" so much that one neglects to love those closest to them. God has designed families as a primary place in which we do his work by loving and caring for one another. It is important not to neglect one's family in pursuit of "the Lord's work."

Being a provider (specifically financially) is the primary job of the husband within traditional gender roles. So long as his family is fed, clothed, and housed, a man may believe he has fulfilled his responsibilities, even if he neglects his family in the process. However, family members have other needs as well. God intends family members to love one another relationally, spiritually, and mentally as well as physically.

Neglect stemming from ministry can be a type of spiritual abuse. When children are neglected in the name of God, they may receive the unspoken message that God does not love them or consider them important. Jesus spoke of God as Father. God intends parents to demonstrate his characteristics to their children. He has given us parents to provide for and love children. In other words, a primary way God intends to love children is through their parents.

James says, "Religion that God our Father accepts as pure and faultless is this: to look after orphans and widows in their distress and to keep oneself from being polluted by the world" (Jas 1:27). Unfortunately, the victims of abuse including spiritual abuse are most often women and children. In the case of neglect, wives and children do technically have husbands and parents. But neglect makes them virtual, hidden widows and orphans.

I can't imagine many things which make God angrier than the women and children he loves being abused. However, one thing would be to do this harm in his name. Spiritual abuse is exactly the opposite of what God wants for people. While those who have experienced spiritual abuse aren't always children biologically, I think Jesus's sentiment applies here.

> If anyone causes one of these little ones—those who believe in me—to stumble, it would be better for them to have a large millstone hung around their neck and to be drowned in the depths of the sea. Woe to the world because of the things that cause people to stumble! Such things must come, but woe to the person through whom they come! (Matt 18:6–7)

Now, I don't know how many—if any—leaders do abusive behavior consciously, so I can't judge their motives. But I have seen the fruit experienced by victims of abuse and trauma done in the name of God, and those whose faith has been destroyed by the kind of unhealthy beliefs and practices talked about in this chapter.

* * *

The subject of spiritual abuse is heavy. Though potentially not as harmful, even in relatively normal churches, sometimes problematic bits can slip into sermons and teachings. It's important to be aware of these in order to be discerning.

Years ago I listened to a sermon by a well-known evangelical pastor. Though I recognized his name, I otherwise knew nothing about him. As I listened, I was shocked by numerous problems in his teaching. His main point actually made sense, but I found his many fallacies and errors particularly concerning.

One relatively minor fallacy he made was to support the use of a word in a broad sense as means of arguing for a very specific use of the word (*equivocation fallacy*). In this case, he referred to preaching and used support for the broad concept of proclaiming a message as proof of the specific need for professional pastors to preach in church services.

Additionally, he criticized churches for not living up to *his own* definition of church. He attacked categories of churches without acknowledging the many ways they *did* fit his description. He used a quote which didn't support his point as though it did. He also used "strawman" arguments, meaning he attacked arguments his opponents did not make. In other words, he misrepresented the position he argued against.

But by far the thing that disturbed me most was his portrayal of anyone who disagreed with him. First, the underlining theme to his words and tone communicated that, if you disagreed with him, not only were you wrong but you were an enemy. The logical conclusion from this was that you should be attacked. Keep in mind, in this teaching he spoke against *other Christians!* Next, he began to make fun of anyone who disagreed with him, as if they were obviously all completely stupid. (This is a form of "gaslighting.") Then finally he said that the people who disagree with him were doing Satan's work and part of cults and sects! To reiterate, he didn't draw a line between those who follow Christ and those who don't. He blatantly called many *fellow servants of God workers of the devil!*

Such behavior harms the cause of Christ. He was clearly passing judgment on fellow believers out of arrogance, essentially placing himself in God's position by claiming to be able to judge people's hearts and know who God accepts and does not accept. This is why Jesus commands us, "Do not judge, or you too will be judged" (Matt 7:1).

I hope this was a slightly extreme example and not common. But I bring this up because you need to be able to spot fallacies like this and not become victim to them. Jesus said, "I am sending you out like sheep among wolves. Therefore be as shrewd as snakes and as innocent as doves" (Matt 10:16) and also, "Watch out for false prophets. They come to you in sheep's clothing, but inwardly they are ferocious wolves" (Matt 7:15).

I believe the pastor I mention above meant well. I think few Christians consciously, intentionally teach what is wrong and/or harmful. Yet we are fallible and therefore can err even if well-intentioned. This is one reason for the body of Christ. If a leader is placed in a position in which he is unchecked, there is no means of countering his mistakes. In contrast, when the church functions as a community, one person's error is more likely to be caught and corrected by another.

I urge you to learn and recognize the fallacies Christian leaders can make. If we are not aware of these things, we become susceptible to beliefs which can either harm our own spiritual health or cause us to behave in ways that harm others' spiritual health.

* * *

Because Christians are fallen just as everyone else, some Christian leaders and churches will behave in ways that harm their congregants' mental, emotional, and spiritual wellbeing. Spiritual abuse in particular happens when a leader or church explicitly or implicitly communicates that God is behind their criticism, displeasure, punishment, or abuse. In order for Christians to be healthy and whole, we need to be aware of what mental, emotional, and spiritual health looks like and the warning signs of those things that are harmful. We must not tolerate such harmful behavior.

The Strength of Jesus

"The foolishness of God is wiser than human wisdom, and the weakness of God is stronger than human strength."
1 Corinthians 1:25

Controversy exists regarding how to imagine Jesus during his earthly life. Some seem to think all other Christians believe Jesus was meek and mild—and they don't like this picture of Jesus. As I discussed in the chapter *Love Is a Verb*, I suppose people think that love means that Jesus can't say no, that he has no backbone, and that any resolve melts in light of emotion. In other words, love is weakness. This is a primary reason people are uncomfortable with the idea of God's love and, therefore, Jesus's love.

Some people have tried to counter their fear of a weak Jesus by attempting to hyper-masculinize Jesus instead. In their minds, the truest picture of Jesus's character occurs when he had a "temple tantrum,"[7] running around with a whip, knocking over tables, and creating a massive scene. By this, they attempt to sanctify aggression. Yes, Jesus did cleanse the temple. He didn't do this dispassionately, but neither did he exhibit out-of-control rage.

Certainly, many men possess more physical strength than emotional tenderness. Many men lean toward achievement, building, working with their hands, shows of physical strength, leadership, etc. And nothing is wrong with this. God made them that way. Yet just as many men do not reflect archetypes of traditional masculinity. Nothing is wrong with men like that either. What *is* wrong is to glorify the stereotype of masculinity, especially aggression.

Phrases such as "real men" clearly imply that any guy who isn't "masculine" enough is a deficient, lesser person who deserves ridicule and disrespect, or at best to be ignored. But holding this position is to commit the sin of condemnation.

Some men who possess more traditionally masculine traits have expressed not feeling welcome in our present society and church.

We as Christians should not participate in this judgment. We shouldn't criticize traditionally masculine men for being the way God created them. Likewise, we shouldn't judge men who aren't as traditionally masculine for being the way God created them. (And we mustn't condemn women for being women, either.)

To counterbalance the above, we also must not use our natural tendencies to justify sin, either. A less traditionally masculine man may be prone to passivity, which can be a sin. However, aggression can be just as much of a sin. In either case, "that's just how I am" is not an excuse.

Those men and women who idealize masculinity have tried to fit Jesus into their own concept of the ideal man. But if Jesus were walking the earth today, you wouldn't find him at the bar watching the game with his bros. Or rather, we might find him in this situation, but not because he couldn't be found elsewhere. In other words, if Jesus were to be seen in a stereotypically masculine setting, it wouldn't be because it was the only setting he felt comfortable in.

Was Jesus weak? Absolutely not. Was he a pushover? Certainly not. Does this mean Jesus was a macho man? Also, no.

[Jesus], being in very nature God, did not consider equality with God something to be used to his own advantage; rather, he made himself nothing   by taking the very nature of a servant, being made in human likeness. And being found in appearance as a man, he humbled himself by becoming obedient to death—even death on a cross (Phil 2:6–8)!

Was it easy for Jesus to choose to come to Earth and become a man? Did he become a servant out of weakness? Was he crucified because he wasn't strong enough to beat his adversaries? No, certainly not.

Jesus worked as a carpenter. In actuality, the original word used means *builder*.[8] Jesus could have been a carpenter, but he was more likely a stonemason, handyman, and/or construction worker. In any case, he was a tradesman, someone who did manual labor and worked with his hands to earn a living prior to his ministry. The vast majority of people in the first century did manual labor, and Jesus was no exception. So one can't say Jesus never worked a hard day, nor was he somehow too tender to do so. Neither was he a privileged, aristocratic elite accustomed to having everything given to him. In this sense, Jesus was a man's man, a man of the people. But, clearly, Jesus was no simpleton.

Jesus wasn't simply the ideal masculine man—he epitomized the ideal man. Or, actually, Jesus expressed the best traits of all humanity.

Using Jesus to idolize masculinity is wrong, just as it's also wrong to use Jesus to idolize the "inspirational" image of Jesus which imagines him as like a sweet old grandma.

It would have been easier for Jesus to stay in heaven. It would have been easier for him to not come to Earth as a baby and live thirty or so years in the first century without our modern conveniences. He could have remained a builder in Nazareth. It would have been easier for him not to challenge the religious establishment and rock the boat, creating waves that would eventually crush him.

But Jesus chose to follow the path the Father had set out for him. He chose to step out and begin teaching. It wasn't easy for Jesus to fast for forty days or be tempted by the devil. It wasn't easy to experience rejection in his home town of Nazareth. It wasn't easy for him to have his life threatened (Luke 4:1–29). It wasn't easy to live for three years constantly traveling and not having a home (Matt 8:20). But Jesus did these things *because* he was strong.

A person may overlook an insult because they wish to avoid conflict. But a person may also overlook an insult out of strength and confidence. Though some people like to think so, aggression is no better than passivity, and vice versa.

Jesus demonstrated fortitude when he went to Jerusalem knowing the fate that awaited him. He entered Jerusalem, taught, and cleansed the temple. He knew these things would cause waves. He didn't do these things out of brash, brazen masculinity but in a sober and measured way. Again, he wasn't an emotionless stoic. But neither did he succumb to hot-headed impulses. He knew exactly what he was doing and what it would cost. This wasn't easy. But Jesus did it anyway *because* of his strength and courage.

A strong, "manly" man may get arrested and executed by powers of the state stronger than himself. Or a man might be too weak to put up a defense. Neither of these were the case for Jesus.

Jesus allowed himself to be arrested. His disciples clearly stood ready to fight. Jesus restrained them, not out of his weakness or timidity, but out of his strength. Imagine the courage it took to allow himself to be arrested knowing torture would soon follow.

Jesus silently refused to defend himself against the accusations made of him at his trial. Was Jesus too weak? Of course not. Instead, he had confidence in his identity, unthreatened by the accusations. And he had the strength and courage to maintain his composure and restrain his response.

To put it another way, Jesus was the type of strong man we can admire. Instead of aggression or masculine dominance. He demonstrated strength to follow God's path, despite its difficulty. In doing so, he became a model for us to follow.

* * *

Jesus had immense strength and fortitude. But the strength he demonstrated wasn't aggressive, domineering, or hyper-masculine. Instead, he exercised his strength by willingly embodying the Father's self-sacrificing love.

What Is Truth?

"I am the way and the truth and the life. No one comes to the Father except through me." John 14:6

"If you hold to my teaching, you are really my disciples. Then you will know the truth, and the truth will set you free." John 8:31–32

"[The devil] was a murderer from the beginning, not holding to the truth, for there is no truth in him. When he lies, he speaks his native language, for he is a liar and the father of lies. Yet because I tell the truth, you do not believe me! Can any of you prove me guilty of sin? If I am telling the truth, why don't you believe me?" John 8:44–46

For years I've heard Christians arguing the idea that truth is relative. "The world tells you that truth is relative, that whatever you want to be true is true for you." This argument never made sense to me. For example, I never thought non-Christians would agree the sky is green if I decide it is. Nor would non-believers say gravity does not exist simply because I decide I don't believe in it.

I finally realized there are different types of truth. Some things are true by virtue of observation and experimentation. Gravity exists. A metal wire conducts electricity. Two plus two equals four. These are facts because we have observed them to be true repeatedly without exception. They are fundamental to the universe no matter what we think or feel about them—or even if we don't think about them at all.

Other things are true by definition. A triangle has three sides. Europe is a continent. These are true because we have designated them as such. A triangle would exist regardless of what we call it, but "a triangle has three sides" is true because we have defined a "triangle" as such.

Each person's experience has a certain truth to it. I feel hungry. I feel lonely. These statements are somewhat irrefutable. I can't tell you how you feel. Or rather, while I could attempt to tell you how you feel, I have no authority or basis for knowing how you feel except for what you share with me. I could say, "You're mean!" because of something you said to me. But perhaps you meant it as a compliment. "That was mean" is not an objective truth in this case. Yet each person's experience is a truth. In other words, it can be true I felt hurt by something you said even while it's also true that what was said was not intended as hurtful.

Still other things are logically true. A classic example from philosophy is: All men are mortal; Socrates is a man; therefore, Socrates is mortal. The conclusion must logically be true if the preceding two statements are true.

The above isn't an all-inclusive list, and we can divide truths up in different ways. The point here is to recognize that different things as true for different reasons.

When Christians talk about absolute versus relative truth, they don't have in mind any of the previously mentioned types of truth. Instead, they are thinking of moral or biblical truth.

The challenge with moral truth is that it is not true in the same way as many of the other truths we have talked about. We have no way to prove a moral proposition is morally correct like we do to prove gravity or a mathematical theorem. We can't prove the existence or nature of God by running experiments. We can't scientifically verify Jesus's teachings.

The argument for moral truth sounds like this: The Bible is wholly correct and everything it says is true. For example, the Bible says, "You shall not murder" (Exod 20:13). Therefore, murder is always wrong for all people at all times in all situations regardless of any other factors. This is an absolute truth. How do we know it is true? Because the Bible says it and does not qualify this rule.

The example logic regarding murder seems reasonably solid, but I will point out a couple of things about it. First, this presumes that the Bible intended a given statement to be understood as a universal truth. The Ten Commandments appear to apply universally. But most would recognize that "When you come, bring the cloak that I left with Carpus at Troas, and my scrolls, especially the parchments" (2 Tim 4:13) is not intended as instruction for everyone. So how do we know which statements in the Bible are intended as universal commands?

In order to uphold the above framework for moral truth, many Christians feel that it is crucial to maintain that everything in the Bible is literally true in every way. Effort is put forth to show that the Bible we have now is essentially as it was originally written, that the correct writings—those inspired by God—are included in the Bible, non-inspired writings are omitted, and that statements in the Bible are historically accurate. Many similarly think of the Bible as effectively "written in stone," meaning that if it states something in one part of the Bible, it must be absolutely true, like a legal document.

I see a couple of problems with this view of the Bible. First, the Bible, and the New Testament in particular, communicates a paradigm which is more about exhibiting virtues than merely following the letter of the law. The Bible isn't a technical, legal document. Instead, it teaches us to walk by the Spirit and describes the general character we will exhibit when we do so (Gal 4:16, 22–23).

Second, in some places the Bible seems to contradict itself. These aren't really problematic unless one takes such a rigid view of the Bible. For example, in the Sermon on the Mount, Jesus states, "I tell you that anyone who divorces his wife, except for sexual immorality, makes her the victim of adultery, and anyone who marries a divorced woman commits adultery" (Matt 5:32). Yet Paul says, "If any brother has a wife who is not a believer and she is willing to live with him, he must not divorce her... But if the unbeliever leaves, let it be so. The brother or the sister is not bound in such circumstances" (1 Cor 7:12, 15). If we look at this in a technical, legal sense, what is the acceptable case for divorce? Jesus gives one case and Paul another, but they're not the same. However, if we understand the Bible less rigidly, the problem dissolves. We understand that both Jesus and Paul discourage divorce though allow it in limited circumstances.

Additionally, the need for the Bible to be completely literal in order to support morality potentially places more weight on the Bible than it should bear. It should go without saying that Jesus and God the Father are greater than the Bible. This means that Jesus is the truth (John 14:6) regardless of the Bible. In other words, Jesus is true even if part of the Bible were to be shown to not be scientifically or historically accurate, or if a portion of scripture is not intended as literally as many

Christians presently understand it. I'm not saying the Bible is necessarily inaccurate or not literal, but merely that these aren't required for the truth of Jesus.

To explore the Bible much more would take us beyond the scope of this chapter. But do not be afraid! I will develop these ideas further in an entire chapter on the Bible.

* * *

Recently, many Christians have become known for their skepticism toward well supported ideas and those who are experts in their field. At the same time, Christians are also becoming known for their belief in ideas that have little evidence and in people who make claims outside of their expertise.

Ironically, these Christians often talk about "truth" more than others do. Some people seem to believe truth is whatever they state it is. They make adamant claims about the truth of the Bible or current events. These people seem to think that being adamant makes a claim true, even though they often cite other evidence. But for something to be true, a reality must exist behind it. One can swear up and down that the moon is made of cheese. But in order for this to be true, to be reality, the moon has to actually be made of cheese when someone lands there. (This is not a claim I've heard anyone make; I'm merely using this example to avoid getting sidetracked by use of a controversial topic.)

Once the evidence clearly demonstrates a person is wrong about a belief they hold, they have a few ways to respond. Some people will acknowledge their error and adjust their beliefs accordingly. Unfortunately, too many people will continue to double down and adamantly insist they are still correct.

Continuing the previous example, we landed, took samples, and clearly demonstrated that the moon is not made of cheese. Yet some will insist the astronauts were mistaken, or they just didn't look in the right place, or that the landing never happened, etc. In other words, they will come up with any and every explanation as to why they are still right.

This kind of thinking presents a significant challenge for Christianity. Jesus stated that he is the truth (John 14:16). In light of this, one would think that Christians would pursue truth. Instead, it reflects poorly on Christianity when many of its adherents believe in something demonstrably untrue. How do we convince others of the truth of Christ if we insist on holding beliefs which are either false or highly unlikely? If I espouse a fringe idea such as that the Earth is flat, non-Christians will likely dismiss what I believe about Jesus as well.

We need to encourage the honest examination of truth claims and learn how to recognize which ideas are well supported and which are unsupported. We need to recognize who speaks with expertise on a subject and who speaks with little knowledge of a topic. Church should be a place that honors truth and gives little notice to false teaching even while respecting every person regardless of their beliefs.

I know very little via my own direct experience. If it were just me, I'd have no idea why objects fall to the ground, why I need to breathe air, what air even is, what stars are, that I am made of trillions of cells, and much, much more. I know these things because of the work of others which has been shared with me. Likewise, I would have little knowledge of Jesus if his teaching hadn't been passed down to me. (Truly, one of the greatest superpowers of humanity is the ability to communicate knowledge through complex language and writing.)

We can also speak of humanity having collective knowledge. Just as our individual knowledge is imperfect, so our collective knowledge is imperfect as well. It can feel like if we don't know something absolutely, then we know nothing at all. This is a false dichotomy. The fact that our knowledge is not completely accurate does not mean we have no knowledge whatsoever.

For most of human history, the vast majority of people have been uneducated. Those who were—generally the civil and religious authorities—told everyone else that they knew what they were talking about and to trust them. The uneducated populace had no grounds for disagreement. Even if they did disagree, they had little chance to voice their opinion or the power to effect change.

This began to change during the Enlightenment. Thinkers of the era began to encourage people to think for themselves and not to trust traditional authorities. Their counsel was made possible by the growing access to published materials and increase in literacy. Gradually, Western culture shifted to individualism, in which the individual is the ultimate authority on truth.

Though it actually predates the Enlightenment, one example of individualism is the Protestant Reformation. The reformers challenged the authority of the Pope and Catholic Church. Though not the only reason, the paradigm that each person is an authority for truth is part of what has led Protestantism to fracture into hundreds of denominations.

It's worth noting that the recent invention of the printing press was a technology that enabled the Reformation. This technology allowed individuals greater ability to disseminate their ideas even if they did not hold social or political power.

In our present day, we've swung to the far end of the spectrum. Now, anyone can relatively easily publish anything they want to say and potentially reach millions of people. Is this good or bad? It's actually mixed. When all knowledge, power, and communication are concentrated in a few people (the king, pope, church, state, et cetera), they hold the power to intentionally mislead people for their own gain. This happened throughout history. The institutions led by monarchs and oligarchs are also prone to stagnation, as they will more likely uphold the status quo even when incorrect or harmful.

Society benefits by having the ability to challenge the authorities and establishment when they become corrupt. It is also positive for people to have the ability to introduce new ideas for consideration. Furthermore, it is great that certain groups that have been outside of positions of authority now have the ability to share their perspectives. We are collectively wiser for this. Society collectively benefits from the greater access people have to learn, think, and share their ideas.

Our time has become known as the "information age." The internet has made an incredible amount of information more easily accessible than ever before. But this has almost as quickly led us to the disinformation age. Tools have the ability to be used for very beneficial purposes, but they can also be used for harm and destruction as well.

Because anyone can easily publish anything on the internet, anyone can pretend to be anyone or represent any group. That headline you see online could be posted by the *New York Times*, your neighbor, a kid in Malaysia, or a Russian-supported operative. Clearly, not all of these sources are equally reliable nor do they likely have the same motives. Therefore, it's critically important that we discern between these sources. (This evaluation of trustworthiness, bias, and motives is known as media literacy.)

The need to separate truth from disinformation also highlights the importance of general consensus. With hundreds of millions of people in the United States, it will always be possible to find some doctor, professor, author, etc. who holds whatever view a person hopes for.

It is true that a new understanding about the world often starts as an uncommon opinion. But not every unusual idea should be accepted as true. The position held by the most experts on a subject—the consensus—is generally the most accurate one.

You may have heard of scholarly journals. No, I don't read any of these, either. But they play an important role in our collective knowledge. Articles published in one of these journals have been "peer reviewed," that is, examined by at least a couple of other *experts on the specific subject at hand*. Though no system is perfect, this prevents a single person with completely baseless ideas from having their ideas spread as though they have probable validity.

What is the point in mentioning scholarly journals if the vast majority of us will never read them? Generally speaking, the ideas that come from these journals will eventually filter down to other experts, such as doctors and professors. And various findings will at times be reported on by the media.

If I need an operation, I want to be certain the procedure is performed by a licensed doctor who has gone through the proper schooling and training. I won't trust my friend to do this no matter how many episodes of *Scrubs* he has watched. I won't even trust a veterinarian despite the similarity in these fields. If I am driving over a bridge, I want to know a licensed civil engineer designed it. If I fly in a plane, I want to be certain it was designed by an aeronautical engineer in consultation with mechanical, electrical, and materials engineers, etc. I won't trust my neighbor to do this job even if he is a trained pilot.

When I go to church, I assume the pastors have a certain amount of education regarding the Bible and living the Christian life. However, I won't seek them for medical advice, at least no more than for anecdotal experience as I might receive from any other person not in the medical profession. I wouldn't expect my pastor to design a bridge nor would I trust him to operate on my pet. And while many pastors have been taught basic "pastoral counseling," I wouldn't go to them for the level of therapy that requires a licensed counselor.

Beliefs have consequences. The more our beliefs align with reality, the more the consequences will be positive. Conversely, when our beliefs are at odds with reality, the more likely the consequences will be negative. If I believe I can walk on water and subsequently try to do so, I will soon find myself soaked. It would be one thing if the consequences of my beliefs only affected me. However, often our beliefs hold consequences for others. If I believe others can walk on water and thus throw them overboard, I may cause them to drown if they are unable to swim.

A core idea in Christianity is that we are to love others similarly to how Jesus would if he were in our position. When Christians espouse false beliefs, we may end up causing harm to others—exactly the opposite of Jesus's love.

* * *

Jesus is truth. As his followers, we ought to pursue truth as well. Christians lose credibility when we promote false beliefs. We may also unintentionally hurt others as well. If we better learn media literacy and how to discern what is likely to be true and what is not, Christians will become more convincing when communicating moral truth and less likely to cause unintended harm.

Hell

"Do not store up for yourselves treasures on earth, where moths and vermin destroy, and where thieves break in and steal. But store up for yourselves treasures in heaven, where moths and vermin do not destroy, and where thieves do not break in and steal. For where your treasure is, there your heart will be also."
Matthew 6:19–21

"Unless you repent, you too will all perish."
Luke 3:3, 5

"[The Lord] is patient with you, not wanting anyone to perish, but everyone to come to repentance." 2 Peter 3:9

The concept of hell is a foundational aspect of many people's paradigm of Christianity. Yet the suggestion that God sends people to be tortured for eternity, a.k.a. hell, is one of the primary reasons people cite as cause for deconstructing their faith and, in some cases, leaving their faith altogether. In this chapter I wish to help strengthen the faith of those who find the common conception of hell challenging.

I don't remember the view ever being described in so many words, but the impression I had of Christianity was essentially the following: God has a somewhat arbitrary list of rights and wrongs. What God has designated as wrong we call sins. In theory, God's rules are for our good. However, we can't know what is good; we can only follow the rules God laid out for us in the Bible. In other words, even if something seems to have bad consequences, we must consider it good if God's rules say so and vice versa. God will judge us based on this list and will let us into heaven if we pass the test, but he will send us to hell if not.

I was certainly taught that our salvation (entrance into heaven) isn't based on our "works" (what we do) but rather solely on Christ's sacrifice. As with the mixed views of God reviewed in chapter 3, this again demonstrates the sometimes confused and contradictory views Christians hold. Protestant theology says that God offers salvation purely based on his grace and mercy and that we do nothing to earn it. Yet Christians preach so much about sin that one gets the impression our salvation is actually conditional on our actions. Many denominations also have such an anemic view of the Holy Spirit that, once we say the "sinner's prayer," it seems it's then up to us to not sin thereafter. No pressure!

With this in mind, along with passages such as that of the sheep and goats (Matt 25:31–46), it's no wonder some Christians are plagued by the terror of going to hell.

But what if God doesn't decide who goes to heaven and who goes to hell based on some semi-arbitrary rules? What if God doesn't send people to heaven or hell at all? What if one's eternal destiny is intrinsically based on what type of person one is? In other words, what if heaven can only be experienced by a certain type of person? Before we begin to answer these questions, let's examine the concept of hell.

Hell, at least as we usually think of it, does not appear in the Bible. To be sure, Jesus did warn people at times to avoid what is translated into English as *hell*. The original concept, however, is very different than the pop-culture image of hell we have today. Our contemporary impressions of hell—a red devil with a pitchfork and demons torturing people in every conceivable way—come more from medieval art and Dante's *Inferno* than they do from the Bible.

Where did the word *hell* originate? In the early medieval period, Anglo-Saxons used the word *hel* for the Latin *īnfernus* when they translated the Bible from that language. This word, *hel,* came from Norse mythology. The old Norse *hel* was the name of the place of fate of evildoers and those who otherwise died dishonorably.[9]

The majority of the verses that are translated as *hell* in English all use the Greek word *gehenna.* This name is a transliteration of a shorthand word in Hebrew which meant "Valley of Hinnom."

In the first century, the Valley of Hinnom was the south and southwest border of Jerusalem, just outside of the city walls. It had been the location of idolatry and child sacrifice (2 Kgs 23:10, Jer 7:31, 19:5–6). It subsequently became known as defiled and cursed.

A somewhat common idea is that the Valley of Hinnom was used as a garbage dump. While fitting, that story is historically unlikely to be true. Nevertheless, during the intertestamental period,[10] *gehenna* developed into the concept of a place of fiery judgment for the wicked. In other words, *gehenna* began to be used symbolically to refer to judgment for evildoers.

Below we'll look at the passages in the New Testament which mention *hell.* However, I've replaced the word *hell* by its most accurate, original language equivalent. First are the passages in the Bible which use *gehenna.*

Do not be afraid of those who kill the body but cannot kill the soul. Rather, be afraid of the One who can destroy both soul and body in the Valley of Hinnom (Matt 10:28).

"I tell you, my friends, do not be afraid of those who kill the body and after that can do no more. But I will show you whom you should fear: Fear him who, after your body has been killed, has authority to throw you into the Valley of Hinnom. Yes, I tell you, fear him" (Luke 12:4).

Again, anyone who says to a brother or sister, "Raca," is answerable to the court. And anyone who says, "You fool!" will be in danger of the fire of the Valley of Hinnom (Matt 5:22).

"Woe to you, teachers of the law and Pharisees, you hypocrites! You travel over land and sea to win a single convert, and when you have succeeded, you make them twice as much a child of the Valley of Hinnom as you are... You snakes! You brood of vipers! How will you escape being condemned to the Valley of Hinnom?" (Matt 23:15, 33).

The tongue also is a fire, a world of evil among the parts of the body. It corrupts the whole body, sets the whole course of one's life on fire, and is itself set on fire by the Valley of Hinnom (Jas 3:6).

If your right eye causes you to stumble, gouge it out and throw it away. It is better for you to lose one part of your body than for your whole body to be thrown into the Valley of Hinnom. And if your right hand causes you to stumble, cut it off and throw it away. It is better for you to lose one part of your body than for your whole body to go into the Valley of Hinnom (Matt 5:29–30).

And if your eye causes you to stumble, gouge it out and throw it away. It is better for you to enter life with one eye than to have two eyes and be thrown into the fire of the Valley of Hinnom (Matt 18:9).

If your hand causes you to stumble, cut it off. It is better for you to enter life maimed than with two hands to go into the Valley of Hinnom, where the fire never goes out. And if your foot causes you to

> stumble, cut it off. It is better for you to enter life crippled than to have two feet and be thrown into the Valley of Hinnom. And if your eye causes you to stumble, pluck it out. It is better for you to enter the kingdom of God with one eye than to have two eyes and be thrown into the Valley of Hinnom, where "'the worms that eat them do not die, and the fire is not quenched'" (Mark 9:43–48).

I don't believe Jesus intends to say that evildoers will be thrown into the literal Valley of Hinnom in Jerusalem. If not literal, then Jesus doesn't give a specific name to or concrete details regarding what we think of as hell. Instead, he paints a picture of an unpleasant fate involving fire for the wicked. This imagery conveys meaning rather than literal details. It is subsequently also uncertain if the fire is intended literally or rather as a symbol of destruction.

In Revelation, John says, "I saw the Holy City, the new Jerusalem, coming down out of heaven from God" (21:2). It's clear the new Jerusalem represents what we call heaven. John goes on to describe the city and its splendor. He then shares, "Nothing impure will ever enter it, nor will anyone who does what is shameful or deceitful, but only those whose names are written in the Lamb's book of life."

With this passage from Revelation in mind, we can understand that Jesus taught that those whose hearts have not been transformed will find themselves outside of his kingdom, excluded from the heavenly city of God.

There are a few more passages related to hell to look at. In Greek mythology, Hades is the name for the land of the dead (as well as the name of the god of this realm). Two passages in the New Testament use the term *Hades*:

The rich man also died and was buried. In Hades, where he was in torment, he looked up and saw Abraham far away, with Lazarus by his side. So he called to him, "Father Abraham, have pity on me and send Lazarus to dip the tip of his finger in water and cool my tongue, because I am in agony in this fire" (Luke 16:22–24).

And I saw the dead, great and small, standing before the throne, and books were opened. Another book was opened, which is the book of life. The dead were judged according to what they had done as recorded in the books. The sea gave up the dead that were in it, and death and Hades gave up the dead that were in them, and each person was judged according to what they had done. Then death and Hades were thrown into the lake of fire.

> The lake of fire is the second death. Anyone
> whose name was not found written in the
> book of life was thrown into the lake of fire
> (Rev 20:12–15).

By using Hades in these passages, I don't think the authors intended to confirm Greek mythology. Additionally, in the passage from Luke, Hades is merely the setting for a story, not the focus of the teaching itself. Caution is warranted in drawing too many conclusions from this type of context.

The passage in Revelation is interesting because of how the author uses death and Hades as objects in verse 14. Normally "death" isn't an object one can throw. Certainly the idea here must not be literal, but rather be intended to poetically describe how death and the realm of the dead will be destroyed.

Note that the text doesn't say anything suggesting death and Hades will be tortured eternally. In fact, saying that "the lake of fire is the second death" actually suggests the lake of fire is a metaphor here—like so many other images in Revelation. In this case, it's a way of saying what is thrown into the "lake" will be destroyed and cease to exist—a second death.

This passage in Revelation is tricky for another reason. At first glance, it looks like people will be judged by what they did. But Protestant Christians believe that we are saved by grace, not by works. If we look closely, we see that one set of books apparently contain a record of people's deeds after which the text mentions the book of life. The people thrown into the lake of fire are those whose names are absent from the book of life. People are spared from this fate, not because of their deeds, but because of their faith in Jesus, symbolized by the record of their names in the book of life.

So what is the judgment here? It could be that those whose names are not found in the book of life will be judged according to their deeds. Or possibly we will all experience a reckoning for our actions, similar to what Paul describes in 1 Corinthians.

> [People's work] will be revealed with fire, and the fire will test the quality of each person's work. If what has been built survives, the builder will receive a reward. If it is burned up, the builder will suffer loss but yet will be saved—even though only as one escaping through the flames (1 Cor 3:13–15).

This passage suggests that the good we do in this life can in some way translate into God's future fulfilled kingdom.

In addition to Hades, Peter refers to Tartarus in one passage:

> For if God did not spare angels when they
> sinned, but sent them to Tartarus, putting
> them in chains of darkness to be held for
> judgment ... (2 Pet 2:4).

Tartarus also appears in Greek mythology as the afterlife destination for the wicked. In this way, it's actually closer than Hades to our concept of hell. Just as with the idea of Hades, Peter wasn't affirming Greek mythology. Instead, he used the closest equivalent his readers would recognize.

Finally, one more passage conjures the image of hell without specifically using one of the words we've reviewed:

> Then he will say to those on his left,
> "Depart from me, you who are cursed, into
> the eternal fire prepared for the devil and
> his angels" (Matt 25:41).

This seems to refer to the same fate as the lake of fire in Revelation.

* * *

Christians hold three primary views of hell: eternal conscious torment, conditionalism or annihilationism, and Christian universalism.

The concept of eternal, conscious torment is the most common view of hell among Protestants today. However, the only passage which suggests conscious torment is the parable of the rich man and Lazarus. Again, I caution against taking too much insight regarding the afterlife from this passage in which the afterlife is only the context for the parable, not the teaching itself. This imagined scene takes place before the final judgment in Revelation, when people are thrown into the "lake of fire." In other words, the scene depicted in the parable cannot be understood as the eternal fate of the rich man.

Mark (9:48) quotes from Isaiah when he says that "the worms that eat them do not die, and the fire is not quenched."

> And they will go out and look on the dead
> bodies of those who rebelled against me;
> the worms that eat them will not die, the
> fire that burns them will not be quenched,
> and they will be loathsome to all mankind
> (Isa 66:24).

Does this mean that all people will literally end up in a place where they can look at all the dead who rebelled against God? It seems more likely that this is poetic language intended to exhort its listeners to follow God rather than rebel against him. Even if it were to be taken literally, we see here *dead* bodies, not living recipients of torture.

The last passage on which eternal torment can rest is that of Matthew 25:31–46. These verses state that the fire is eternal. However, it doesn't state that what is thrown into the fire will continue to burn eternally. We can assume the fire would consume whatever is thrown into it as fires typically do. In this case, the concept of the fire as eternal could be meant to convey the idea that the destruction caused by the fire will be eternal, and anyone so consumed will never recover. In other words, their destruction is eternally lasting, not eternally in process.

Annihilationism is the name given to this view which asserts that the fate of those who do not possess eternal life will be eternal death. In other words, these people will stay dead eternally—their death will be final. It does not mean they will remain eternally in the process of dying somehow forever frozen in the middle of the process. (Conditionalism is essentially the same, asserting that people are by nature mortal and that immortality is only conditionally conferred on those who are saved.)

The last view, "Christian universalism," likely sounds concerning to many. After all, universalism is often known as "all roads lead to heaven," which stands in contrast to the claim that Jesus is the only way. *Christian* universalism, however, teaches that in the end, God will save everyone. Some Christians have come to this view as they try to take seriously the truth that God truly loves everyone and that his love is powerful.

Christian universalism is Christian in contrast to "general" universalism because those who hold it believe that God saves everyone *through Jesus.* Essentially, Christian universalists hold all the regular beliefs about God and Jesus. The only difference is that they believe God will eventually save everyone from hell. This could mean that no one is sent to hell in the first place, or it could be that some go to hell for a period but are eventually saved.

Why have I taken the time to examine hell and the views Christians hold? I want you to know what the Bible says and doesn't say about it. It's also good to understand that not all Christians have the same belief about hell. In other words, you don't have to believe in a hell of eternal conscious torment in order to be a Christian. True, some Christians may accuse anyone who doesn't hold to this view of hell as not being Christian. Fortunately, they do not control your eternal destiny—God does. And he loves you!

* * *

The specter of hell haunts many believers. One passage that worries some Christians is that of the "unforgivable sin." They fear they might accidentally commit the unforgivable sin and therefore be beyond God's power to redeem. In this passage, Jesus famously says that blasphemy against the Holy Spirit will not be forgiven.

> When the Pharisees heard [about Jesus's healing], they said, "It is only by Beelzebul, the prince of demons, that this fellow drives out demons" (Matt 12:24).

> Jesus said to them, "...Every kind of sin and slander can be forgiven, but blasphemy against the Spirit will not be forgiven" (Matt 12:31).[11]

This passage has confused and greatly concerned many people. Yet within the context, it's not difficult to understand. Jesus makes this comment in response to the religious leaders who observe the miracles Jesus is doing but who attribute them to Satan instead of God.

The point here is that if people can't recognize God when he is immediately in front of them, what more can God do? *Nothing.*

Heaven is the place where God's ways are reality. But if one thinks God's ways are Satan's, then could they experience heaven even if they were there? Clearly not. They would perceive themselves to be in the domain of the devil—in hell.

Earlier in the chapter, I posed some questions regarding hell and judgment. This included the question, "What if heaven can only be experienced by a certain type of person?" I love the scene in C. S. Lewis's *The Last Battle* that I think perfectly illustrates the idea. During a battle, one of the characters enters a stable only to find that inside is "heaven." Some dwarves were also thrown into the same stable. However, though they are in "heaven," they can't see it—they think they are still trapped in the dark, dirty stable![12]

Am I saying that heaven and hell are merely states of mind? No. But what I am saying is that the notion that God *sends* people to heaven or hell makes much less sense than what I just described. God isn't arbitrarily and casually deciding people's eternal fate based on his mood. God isn't like a crotchety old schoolmaster grading papers, heartlessly marking down any technical error. He doesn't hope someone will commit the unforgivable sin so he can mercilessly condemn them with a menacing laugh. This describes the archetypical evil villain—not the good God of the universe! He is the God who came into the world to love the world, not to condemn it (John 3:17). The idea that Jesus came to teach us how to be people who can experience the goodness of his kingdom is so much more amazing.

* * *

It is most common to understand Jesus's death as an atoning sacrifice for people's sins. While the Bible does teach this, there is more than one aspect to this most important event in human history.

An important part of Jesus's ministry was how he demonstrated what it looked like to live out God's ways as a human being. People have always had beliefs regarding what they think God must be like. However, they often make God out to be more human-like—petty and fickle—than he is. Jesus came in part to set the record straight. One of the most important ways he did this was through his death.

The Jews expected a warrior Messiah, a general who would free them from Roman occupation. Jesus clearly didn't meet these messianic expectations. Instead, Jesus certainly appeared to have lost and failed. But Jesus's death wasn't a mistake. Instead, through it Jesus demonstrated God's mind-blowing power.

Violence begets violence. People usually think that destroying their enemies is the only path to peace, security, and prosperity. In contrast, violence, hatred, and actions motivated by anger usually just perpetuate more of the same. If one enemy is destroyed, another will always be perceived. There will never be an end to the fear and felt need to eliminate another threat.

Jesus didn't gather an army to fight the Romans. He didn't even overthrow the Jewish religious and political establishment. He didn't counter his enemies by destroying them. Instead, Jesus allowed his enemies to do their worst to him.

We considered Jesus's strength in chapter 5. Jesus exhibited immense toughness and tenderness. Jesus wasn't passive or too weak to stand tough in the face of controversy. He wasn't arrested because he was powerless to resist. On the contrary, it took incredible strength and fortitude to *allow* himself to be the subject of unjust violence without fighting back. Again, his crucifixion wasn't a mistake. Jesus knew that hatred and violence can't be overcome with even more hatred and violence. He knew that love and peace aren't obtained through hatred and violence.

The powers of evil unleashed their worst on Jesus: torture and death. What more could violence do beyond this?

From Satan's point of view, the greatest victory imaginable had just been won. God's own Son—a member of God himself—had just been killed. Because we know the end of the story, it's easy to overlook this part. But pause for a moment to consider the Saturday between Jesus's crucifixion and resurrection.

How would you have felt if you were one of Jesus's disciples? By the world's standards, the violence of evil had defeated Jesus and the ways of God which he represented. Can we imagine any scenario worse for God and better for evil? It was a dark day indeed!

But of course this wasn't the end of the story. God's power is so great, he took what appeared to be the worst thing that could happen and used it as the lynch pin in his plan to redeem the world. God raised Jesus from the dead. The powers of evil had exhausted their power. Jesus overcame the violence of evil through self-sacrificial love. Love wins!

Jesus came to demonstrate how to be the type of person who will experience heaven. It's not the type of person with a "worldly" mind who sees others as the enemy to be defeated. Those who understand that God so loved the world—all people—are the ones who are able to participate in God's kingdom. And part of being his children means demonstrating that we love others, too.

Loving others can seem difficult, especially in the face of those who seem to be fighting against us. Yet Jesus demonstrated once and for all that God's power is greater than the evils of violence. The martyrs of early Christianity demonstrated this. We have the power through God to love even in the face of death and punishment because we know Jesus resurrected and God will vindicate us as well.

The penal substitutionary view of Jesus's death suggests that Jesus—God the Son—saves us from the wrath of God the Father. However, God is absolutely not divided within himself. What I have described in the latter part of this chapter is essentially the "Christus victor" view which was more popular in early Christianity. It understands Jesus as having beaten *the forces of evil* as opposed to the anger of the Father.

God understood that only a certain type of person, one who has the correct view or sees correctly, can experience the kingdom of God. Jesus came to Earth and suffered in order to show us God's ways. He went to this immense length in order to save us, out of his love for us!

We were bound by the forces of evil and to the forces of evil. Jesus had to demonstrate the only way out of these chains and to the Father.

To me, this understanding of Christ's sacrifice is mind-blowingly amazing! It certainly borders on incomprehensible. Only God, in his unfathomable wisdom and understanding, could orchestrate such salvation!

In this chapter, it may have sounded as though I am shifting the burden of our salvation from God to ourselves. This is not the case. We don't do anything to earn our salvation. All we do is accept the path Jesus has shown us. We only have to walk in faith. And God does not leave us alone here, either. He gives us his Spirit, who empowers us to walk in faith.

* * *

Many Christians hold hell as a "stick" required for the message of Christianity. The popularity of this view is understandable because it's a simple formula which uses fear as motivation. And we know fear is often an effective way of motivating people.

However, this take on the gospel unfortunately seems to place more emphasis on what God is saving us *from* rather than what good God is saving us *for*.

A common means of evangelism looks like this: First convince a person they are a sinner according to the Bible, next convince them they deserve punishment (hell) due to their sin, then finally offer the "good news" for this predicament we just now sold them. "No worries! Jesus saves! Simply confess your belief in him and you won't go to hell!"

I have a problem with this "gospel." It just doesn't seem to me to be such great news when I first had to be convinced that I am so bad that I deserve eternal torment. I know some people feel a sense of their own badness viscerally. But for me, it has always been too abstract to feel even if I believed it in my head.

However, this bad news formula is unnecessary. Though people are told they only need to confess to be saved, many churches focus on imploring people not to "sin." In practice, this too frequently means acting culturally conservatively rather than biblically moral. Sure, fear can be used to coerce people into behaving a certain way. But the true gospel is about more than scaring people into "clean-cut" behavior.

Do you remember that the Gospels say that Jesus went around preaching the good news?[13] What was the good news that Jesus was preaching? Did he preach, "Believe in my death as an atoning sacrifice so that I won't send you to hell when you die"? This wouldn't have made any sense before his resurrection. Instead, he preached the good news that God's kingdom was arriving.

Why is this good news? What does God save us to? Remember that Paul tells us in Galatians that the evidence of God's Spirit is love, joy, peace, patience, kindness, goodness, faithfulness, gentleness, and self-control (5:22–23). God is good, perfectly loving, just, merciful, and more. God's kingdom is the realm where his ways and his characteristics are fully expressed.

The miracles Jesus performed weren't just tricks to demonstrate his power. No, his miracles were a demonstration of what his kingdom is like. People are healed! People are free! Sinners are loved. Even the dead receive life! In a word, all of the wrongs of the world are healed and made right. Who doesn't want this to be true?

Common pictures of heaven are as off base biblically speaking as images of hell. The kingdom of God doesn't consist of us floating on clouds surrounded by harp playing angels. Instead, imagine all of the beauty of the world, the good people, the leaves in fall, flowers, mountains, a sunny day, animals, streams. Imagine all of this part of the world but with none of the bad. No poverty, war, famine, hate, sorrow, or death. Imagine we have all the time to enjoy our friends and families, all the time to travel or paint or golf or whatever we most enjoy. God created us with a purpose and gave us different talents. In heaven, we'll have ample time to exercise our gifts, to follow our passions, to interact, travel the world, enjoy all the beauty, to create, and more! Paul, quoting from Isaiah, says that no mind has conceived of what God has prepared for us (1 Cor 2:9, Isa 64:4), but it will certainly be similar in character to what I just described.

The Hebrew word *shalom* is generally translated as *peace*, but the meaning behind *shalom* includes more than simply lack of conflict. It could be better understood as *communal well-being*. It's not just a personal state nor merely the absence of war. It is all of this and more. The kingdom of God will fully incarnate *shalom*.

In our individually focused Western culture, we have looked at the gospel only in terms of the individual as well. People are individually guilty, individually condemned, and individually rewarded or punished.

Not all cultures share this individualistic viewpoint, including the Jews of the first century. Jesus preached the good news *of the kingdom*. God was in their midst, not saving a bunch of individuals from their personal torment in hell but inaugurating his kingdom—the kingdom of God!

This vision of God's kingdom is one I can get behind. This is a vision worth striving for. While we can't usher in God's kingdom ourselves, God has us here on Earth to demonstrate the reality of his kingdom by living out his ways in the world. We are to be this city on a hill, this light in the darkness (Matt 5:14–16)[14]. We witness to the reality of God's kingdom in tangible ways and invite people to join in.

* * *

Hell isn't as clearly defined in the Bible as our cultural imaginations of a red devil with a pitchfork suggest. And it's biblically plausible to think that God does not send people to hell. For one, it's much more in character to understand Jesus as saving us from evil rather than saving us from the Father. The truly important point is to be a kingdom-type person so as not to be left out of Jesus's kingdom. Jesus saves us from the ways of evil in order to transform us into people who can experience and participate in the goodness of God's kingdom.

Washes Whiter Than Ash

"Therefore, there is now no condemnation for those who are in Christ Jesus." Romans 8:1

"If we confess our sins, he is faithful and just and will forgive us our sins and purify us from all unrighteousness." 1 John 1:9

Now that we talked about hell, let's talk about one of the most likely actions to send you there—sex! I jest, but it often seems that Christians are more concerned with this sin than just about anything else. In this chapter, I want to consider Christianity's passion for purity. We can apply the concept of purity to a variety of aspects of life; however, in Christianity, *purity* most often means sexual purity.

Evangelicals are obsessed with sex. It's ironic to say this because Christians have a reputation for their strict prohibitions regarding sex. This might lead one to describe them as anything other than sex obsessed. In reality, evangelicals have been obsessed with trying to *prevent* people—especially teens—from engaging in sex. Christians thought that secular culture was obsessed with sex, idolizing it as the pinnacle of life. (This is true for some people, though less so for others.) Evangelicals swung to the other side and felt compelled to be equally obsessed with preventing people from having sex.

Not all churches emphasized the topic of sex to the same degree, and it seems that now days many churches rarely talk about it at all. Nevertheless, evangelicals hold a conservative sexual ethic. The message of this chapter still applies even if your experience has been somewhat different.

All of the exhortations against sex didn't mean that Christians weren't thinking about or desiring sex. We are curious about sexuality, especially when we do not receive adequate information and when the topic is shrouded in mystery and silence.

I like to call the impulse behind purity culture "the evangelical fear of sex." But the fear seemed to go beyond reasonable concern regarding sex to something like paranoia. If young people had sex, people feared, this would somehow spell certain doom. The consequences of sex were often blown way out of proportion and potentially did more harm than good.

I've heard a joke that Baptists prohibit sex because it might lead to dancing. People laugh because it flips things around and captures the true paranoia regarding sex. Not only is sex prohibited, but many other activities are avoided as well out of fear that they might lead to sex outside of marriage.

Before we go further, and in order to understand how we got here, let's first look back at both the Bible and Christian history.

* * *

I want to start by reviewing the Bible's teachings on sex. This will by no means be comprehensive, but we will hit the most important points.

Christians have rightly been criticized for being unbalanced in regards to which sins they emphasize versus which they do not. In theory, sins other than sex could make one impure, yet only sex was discussed in purity culture. The church has often demonized sexual sin while largely ignoring others such as greed, pride, slander, and gluttony.

However, if one does an inventory of all the "sin lists" in the New Testament, one will discover that sexual sins are mentioned more than any other. So, Christians prioritize sexual purity, in part, honestly.

The Old Testament contains a number of "laws" regarding sexuality, while the New Testament also includes teachings regarding sexuality as well. Before we look at the latter, remember that the New Testament isn't intended to create a new list of rules that believers are required to follow. Instead, the New Testament teaches character and living by the Spirit. So, for example, when Paul lists "the acts of the flesh" in Galatians 5 and conversely the "fruit of the Spirit," these aren't meant as an exhaustive list of rules but rather examples of what good and bad "fruit" look like.

Paul uses several different Greek words related to sexuality in his sin lists. Nearly half of these communicate a prohibition against unrestrained debauchery, orgies, and the like. Adultery is mentioned a couple of times. Another half refer to prostitution and general sexual immorality.

For me, in the twenty-first century, the latter is frustratingly vague. What is immorality in terms of sex? I want a concrete definition! But within the Bible, an understanding of what this meant seems to be a presumed.

Acts 15 describes a council held in Jerusalem in order to decide how Jewish non-Jews needed to be in order to be Christians. They sent a letter to gentile Christians, saying:

> It seemed good to the Holy Spirit and to us not to burden you with anything beyond the following requirements: You are to abstain from food sacrificed to idols, from blood, from the meat of strangled animals and from sexual immorality. You will do well to avoid these things (vv. 28–29).

Note how the church leaders instructed gentile Christians not to engage in sexual immorality. They did not spell out exactly what this meant, but it seems clear by the context that they had the Old Testament in mind. Leviticus 18 in particular contains mostly prohibitions regarding sex. I won't quote the entire chapter here, but the prohibitions are primarily against incest, adultery, bestiality, and the like. Overall, the Bible seems to teach sex is permissible primarily within a marriage.

So if the prohibitions on sex are biblical, what else is there to talk about? Good question! It's the *absence* of teachings regarding sex beyond just the restrictions that have led to problems.

Let me give an example from my own life. Many years into my adult life I remained single despite desiring marriage. As I pondered this, I had a realization. I had always been very cautious around women, especially in terms of flirting or expressing attraction directly. What I realized is that I was waiting for a sense of *permission* from the girl/woman. We've all heard about the fear of rejection in regards to asking a woman out. But my fear went beyond this because of the unbalanced messages I received which only taught what not to do. I had gotten the unconscious idea that rejection would not only sting, but it would mean I had done something *morally wrong* and was therefore a bad person—the worst thing to a Christian. Needless to say, I hardly ever took any initiative. And in a culture in which the guy is expected to initiate and lead, it's no wonder I didn't have any success starting a relationship.

To anyone not familiar with purity culture, this probably sounds crazy—and it is. But it is just one example of the unintended results due to the unbalanced message of purity culture.

The Bible's teachings regarding sexual moderation are important. However, prohibitions alone do not make for comprehensive sex education. We'll look at this more in the next chapter. But before that, let's briefly look at some of the history behind the church's views on sex.

* * *

Sex has been a core issue in Christianity since the beginning. Augustine, arguably the most influential Christian theologian in the West after Paul, had issues with sex. I'm not saying that Christianity's teachings on sex started with Augustine, but he nevertheless had a massive influence. Augustine believed sexual passion—sexual desire itself—was evil. Where did Augustine get this notion from?

In the fourth century B.C., Alexander the Great led his Greek army on a grand quest that saw them take control over the areas from Greece south to Egypt and across the entire Middle East, including Israel—the largest empire the world had yet known. In the wake of this adventure, Greek culture spread wide and their ideas significantly influenced those living in these areas. Though the Romans eventually took control over these areas, Greek ways of seeing the world (Greek philosophy) were still prevalent.

As early as the second century A.D., Jews no longer comprised the majority of Christians. Instead, the majority of Christians were gentiles from the Roman Empire. And again, everyone was influenced by Greco-Roman culture. It was the air they breathed.

Cynic philosophers (a group of Greek thinkers—not just cynical old men) taught that a person could gain happiness through living "naturally"—depending on only the most minimal of possessions. They also taught that living in hardship helped one detach from the world.

Stoic philosophers (another group of Greek thinkers) held that a person should become indifferent to what happened in life. In other words, happiness would come through living *rationally* rather than *passionately*. Therefore, a person would gain greater happiness by detaching from their desires. If they did this, one would consequently also remain content with few possessions.

The Greeks weren't the first to try asceticism. But again, Greek thinking was the thinking of the Greco-Roman world, especially for those who weren't Jewish. Even the Jews had Philo, who attempted to harmonize Judaism with Hellenistic (Greek) thought.

The Greek philosopher Plato had theorized that there must be another reality of ideas. He realized that we identify many different, non-identical things as being the same type of thing. For instance, we identify many different types of objects as a table or many different animals as a cat. This is also true of concepts such as love and beauty. He thought there must be a realm of perfect "forms" in which there exist the perfect table, the perfect cat, etc. Plato held that this realm must be greater than the physical reality we live in. He believed that in the physical world, we remembered these perfect forms we knew before birth. Consequently, Plato imagined we had a soul which could be separated from our body and that was eternal, in contrast to our body. As a result, he held the soul to be more important since it was more permanent than our physical bodies.

During early Christianity, there were several adjacent religious movements which borrowed ideas from Greek thought including Gnosticism[15] and Manicheism.[16] Prior to becoming the theologian we know, Augustine was influenced by Gnosticism and was actually Manichean before he converted to Christianity. The Manicheans believed that sexual desire was innately evil. And though Augustine left Manicheism, he obviously continued to share their views of sex.

Augustine was also influenced by Platonism. And if you separate one's physical body and believe it to be lesser (as with Platonism), then one's natural desires seem to just get in the way of "higher," spiritual pursuit of God. Augustine regretted not being able to control his body, especially in not being able to prevent erection. Though he had a long term mistress before becoming a Christian, once he became a theologian, he held that sexual desire was sinful.[17] He taught that celibacy was ideal, though allowed sex as acceptable only for procreation. This is the root of Roman Catholics opposition to contraception which continues to this day. *Seriously.* Part of our modern-day controversy over healthcare in the U.S. has to do with the beliefs of this man who lived 1,600 years ago!

Before we finally address purity, we need to briefly grasp two additional concepts.

* * *

Evangelical Christians will state that sex is good within marriage. Yet this truth gets overwhelmed by the emphasis on prohibitions. I may mentally ascent to the idea that sex is good in marriage, but in practice be very uncomfortable with the subject in any way. The way evangelicals shun sex in movies, music, and books reveals how we feel negatively about this subject. When we don't talk about sex positively, we implicitly imply that sex is taboo. Furthermore, it seems that churches have become hesitant to talk about it either. None of this helps to alleviate the sense of taboo that many parents grew up with and continue to feel.

Taboos are social norms enforced through negative social consequences for those who violate them. At its mildest, one who brings up the subject may be met with awkward silence and strange looks. A person may also be reprimanded or be shunned in other ways—especially if they make repeated faux paus.

An effect of taboos, perhaps even their purpose, is that they are a way in which people can identify themselves with a group. We all need to belong, and this social connection is important for all of us. This is why social enforcement is so powerful. People will keep themselves in line if they realize that infractions will ostracize them. This is especially true if the group possessing the taboo is a person's sole community or at least the community in which they find their primary identity.

Whether explicitly stated or implicitly implied, a taboo—whether a forbidden word, topic, or behavior—communicates that the subject is terrible, repulsive, evil, or horrendous. Specifically when it comes to sex, it is common for incongruity to exist between what we say we believe and what we feel and subsequent act on. We can therefore possess a negative perception of sex even if we believe we have a positive view of it.

Shame is a kind of self-judgment. Jesus instructed us not to judge others, not to evaluate a person's worthiness. Shame, at least in part, judges *oneself* as not worthy of respect, dignity, etc. A person can feel shame in regards to a certain aspects of themselves while not experiencing it in regards to others. For instance, a person could have self-respect professionally while also experiencing shame regarding their relationships.

Shame and taboo are interlinked. If a person is told implicitly or explicitly that sex is bad, even including sexual desire, when they experience these natural longings, they may internalize this to mean they are therefore bad. This could be a conscious thought, though it doesn't have to be. Often we are affected by impressions such as these even when we aren't fully aware of them.

People will argue that shame is good and that people should feel ashamed when they do something bad such as steal. This depends in part on what we mean when we talk about shame. If a person steals, it seems appropriate they feel ashamed. We don't want them to feel proud of it! Instead, we think they should feel a sense of regret regarding what they did. So what's wrong with shame?

Guilt and shame have been used more or less interchangeably. Yet, well-known author Brené Brown separated them into two nuanced meanings. According to Brown, guilt is recognizing that I have done something bad, whereas shame is believing that I am bad.[18] In other words, guilt occurs when I recognize I have done something wrong and regret having done so. I can choose to right the wrong and do the right thing in the future. I may suffer consequences as a result of my action, but I am otherwise no less deserving of basic respect and dignity. Shame, however, happens when I think I did something bad because I am fundamentally flawed. I deserve not only the consequences of my actions but mistreatment more generally because I am unworthy.

* * *

A push for abstinence which was especially targeted at Christian youth gained popularity in the 1990s. This movement waned after the 2000s, but its influence is still felt. In retrospect, this movement came to be referred to as "purity culture." Though this label has been placed on a specific movement, the idea of purity was not new, nor has it died out. Understanding purity culture can be tricky due to its mix of good and bad messages, and often the messages that had the most impact were not the ones directly spoken.

In their zeal to keep teens from sex, evangelical leaders and parents swung far to the opposite end of the pendulum. They implored youth not just to be abstinent until marriage, but to stay as far away from anything related to sex as possible. Some went as far as to idealize not even touching one's partner until one's wedding!

This movement became known as purity culture because, in their pursuit of preventing teen sex, Christian leaders idealized virginity and the concept of "purity." Effectively, the further away a person stayed from anything sexual, the purer they supposedly were.

To be sure, engaging in sex brings dangers and potential consequences, both physical and emotional.

And there are good reasons for wanting to prevent teen pregnancy. So I believe the motives behind purity culture's desire to limit teen sex were good and the results were not all bad. Yet "purity culture" is perhaps one aspect of Christianity that has caused the most harm as well, even if unintentionally.

I partially understand that evangelical leaders and parents felt as though they were swimming upstream and fighting the massive tide of culture. Therefore, they felt like they had to strongly emphasize abstinence in order to stand a chance of countering the culture. But a result was that many kids who grew up in evangelical culture received only anti-sex messages. In other words, they received a significantly unbalanced teaching regarding sexuality.

In the Sermon on the Mount, Jesus says that whoever looks at a woman lustfully is guilty of sin (Matt 5:27–28). What is lust? For many in purity culture, even just thinking about, desiring, or—heaven forbid—fantasizing about sex constituted lust and therefore sin—at least so long as one didn't banish the thought as soon as it came to mind. (Make sure to "bounce your eyes" and slap that rubber band around your wrist![19])

I never had the words for this at the time, but recently it occurred to me that evangelicals effectively idealized *asexuality*—people who do not experience sexual desire. Yes, Christians would say that sex within marriage is good. However, when sex is primarily talked about in terms of *not* engaging in it, when seeing nudity in any form of media is considered bad and is prohibited, when any mention of sex in music warrants an explicit label, when it's mostly unacceptable to say the names of certain body parts, sexuality comes across as inherently bad. Many Christian couples unfortunately discovered that this sense of "badness" surrounding sex did not suddenly disappear after their wedding vows.[20]

In order to emphasize abstinence, sexual activity was painted with a very dark brush. It was suggested that engaging in sexual activity made a person less lovable and less able to love. There were common object lessons in which an impure person was compared to a chewed-up piece of gum, a flower with all of the petals pulled off or a sticker that had lost its stickiness.

At the beginning of the book we examined fear. Purity culture is an example of an entirely reasonable fear, the potential consequences of sex, which was allowed to grow unreasonably, leading to actions with harmful consequences: the shame and self-condemnation of many young people.

Earlier in the chapter, we saw that the Bible seems to teach sex is permissible primarily within marriage. One may wonder, if the prohibitions on sex are biblical, how could the push for purity go wrong? After all, we can't go wrong doing the right thing, correct?

It's one thing to encourage people to take or refrain from some act from the present onward. But it doesn't make any sense to try to tell people to behave differently in the past. Obviously no one can go back and change anything that has already transpired. Yet the message of purity culture forcefully implied this desire.

The critical error of purity culture came in teaching that, if a person had some kind of sexual experience in the past, that person was forever lesser, broken, dirty, and impure and unworthy of dignity, respect, desire, and love. This would be true *even if the sex was non-consensual!* Once a person "lost" their (sexual) "purity," they could never fully regain it. There was no redemption. No one taught that sex was unforgivable in the sense of God barring a person from salvation. It was just that the *consequences in this life* were taught to be such that impurity was effectively an unforgivable sin.

Along with condemning those who had some kind of sexual experience, purity culture implicitly taught young people that virginity was of utmost importance and would make more of a difference in marriage than it actually does. The unspoken but clear implication: those who had experienced sex outside of marriage were lesser and undesirable potential partners. Of course, not everyone took this to heart, but many Christian youth did, including this author.

I hope it is obvious to you that this message is completely antithetical to the gospel. The good news of Jesus *is redemption*. Remember, God used what seemed to be the worst, irreversible tragedy—the death of his Son—and he shrugged it off. I mean, he didn't take it casually, of course, but he wasn't in a panic. He is more powerful. He's got this. The notion that sexual activity imparts permanent dysfunction on its participants is a lie from Satan. We can be certain of this not only because it contradicts Jesus's message of redemption, but we also know recognize its fruit.

Let's not confuse consequences with the kind of condemnation I am talking about here. It's true that sex has consequences. Secular scholar Helen Fisher has said that no sex is casual (unless one is too drunk to remember it).[21] Sex is significant, has emotional and potential physical consequences, and poses certain risks. But regardless of any consequences, *sexual experience does not make you any less worthy of love and respect.*

Leaders of purity culture may not have intended this message. But in their zealousness to prevent teen sexuality, they employed the use of terror in hopes of scaring the sex out of young people. Of course, this notion that sex was effectively the unforgivable sin wasn't the only thing purity culture taught. But it was perhaps the most impactful side effect.

Acting in an upright way in regards to sex is good and generally leads to health. But this doesn't mean your life is ruined if you have had experiences outside of God's ideal plan. God can bring life and health to you despite anything you have previously experienced.

Just after Jesus makes the statement about lust, he goes on to address divorce (Matt 5:31–32). Some Christians have gotten the idea that sex equals marriage.

Now it is true that marriage is understood as the appropriate setting for sex, and God probably doesn't care as much about the legal certificate of marriage as he does people's vows. However, marriage is much more than sex, and having sex does not mean that God sees you as married forever after in a way that not even divorce can change.

This is important to emphasize because more than one Christian has believed that after their first sexual encounter, they must try to marry the person and make the relationship work. This has been true regardless of the character of the partner, or *even if the sex was non-consensual.* God cares more about you (and the other person) than he does in a rule. In other words, even if God does hate divorce, it doesn't mean he is blind to the fact that some marriages end. Believing that sex equates to marriage has led to some bizarre results, such as a person praying that their ex will have sex with someone (adultery) so that God will finally see them as divorced.

* * *

Purity culture affected girls and women more deeply than it did boys and men for a variety of reasons. As a man, I of course didn't directly experience the effects of purity culture the way girls did. My knowledge has come from listening to the experience of women I know personally as well as those I have read or heard speak.

First of all, people have believed that virginity is more physically embodied in women than in men (though the actual biology of this is questionable). Virginity has been taken as an indicator of a woman's purity. So girls might worry they would be found anatomically deficient in a way that boys could not experience.

In addition to this, it is obvious (at least after several months) if a woman is pregnant and, by deduction, that she has engaged in sex. In contrast, no outward sign (save for modern genetic testing) indicates when a man has engaged in sexual activity. As a consequence, women have more reason to fear being caught after sexual intercourse than men. *The Scarlet Letter* is a perfect example of this point.[22]

Our society is much more egalitarian now than it used to be. Yet we remain affected by the time when women had greater barriers to any sort of leadership, influence, or even working outside of the home. When women had limited opportunities outside the home, her position in life was significantly determined by the man she would marry. In this context, anything which jeopardized her marriageability such as lack of "purity" had real consequences. And though women aren't as dependent on marriage today, I suspect this sense still lingers to some degree. Even if this isn't the case, many girls dream of marriage and kids. Traditionally, men are expected to initiate a relationship with a woman. If a woman believes herself to be undesirable, it could be particularly devastating because it means not just being disliked, but threatens a complete collapse of her expectations and dreams for her life.

Being labeled as sexually impure can hold greater social consequences for women, especially in Christian communities. And a woman who is believed to have had sexual experience can be seen as a danger out of fear that she will tempt other men.

Additionally, in recent history we have been taught that men are more sexual than women. For example, churches typically point to pornography as almost entirely a man's struggle. Therefore, if a woman experiences routine sexual temptation, she could believe she is somehow more broken, unnatural, and less feminine—with the corresponding sense of shame.

(While men on average have a higher sex drive, this significantly varies across people. Research suggests that given a random man and woman, the woman will have a greater sexual drive than the man a third of the time.[23] So having a high or low sex drive does not make a woman unnatural or unfeminine.)

Think about the terms used for a woman who is sexual: *naughty, dirty, bad girl*. These are the opposite of what Christian young women want to be. So many young people deeply desire to do what is right and follow God's way as completely as possible. They fully embraced the message of waiting until marriage. Yet they also believed the message that they effectively couldn't be forgiven if they experienced some kind of sexual activity. This would be true whether or not it had happened before the person heard the gospel or *even if the sexual act wasn't consensual.*

Susan was a Christian woman and longtime proponent of purity. However, in her early adulthood, she ended up having sex. After this happened, she didn't think she deserved a decent relationship because she wasn't "pure." This belief led her to experience further unhealthy sexual encounters that culminated in an abusive relationship. Her self-worth was so low that she stayed in this relationship for a long time. She didn't believe she deserved *not* to be abused. This is one example of the evil effects of sexual shame stemming from purity culture.

Does God feel his precious daughter deserves abuse? Absolutely not! Instead, it is the devil who is thrilled about the anguish and chaos these beliefs brought about.

Sam and Whitney immediately hit it off when they met. They had a lot in common and soon fell in love. They were both Christians influenced by purity culture. However, not long before they had met, Whitney had been raped. As a result, she didn't believe that Sam would love her. She knew that Sam had not had sex and believed he wouldn't want to be in a relationship with a woman who had (despite it not being her choice). So despite their mutual attraction, Sam and Whitney never ended up dating. Instead, Whitney ended up in a series of relationships with men who were more interested in using her body than they were in truly loving her. Sam was broken-hearted and struggled to find love long after. Though the situation was more complex, the messages of purity culture played a leading role in preventing what might have been a godly marriage.

Once again, Jesus stated that we can know a tree by its fruit. The stories I just shared are *not* examples of the kind of abundant life Christ brings. No, these are examples of rotten fruit from the pit of hell.

* * *

Another subject which went hand-in-hand with purity culture was the concept of modesty. Of course the subject of modesty extends well beyond purity culture, both backwards in time and beyond Christianity. For instance, Islam is also well known for how its strict adherents desire to cover women to a large degree. The conversation regarding modesty has nearly exclusively been in relation to women; we almost never talk about how men should be modest. It's another burden which has been placed on women in a way which men do not experience.

In mental health, there is a crucial concept called boundaries. It's critical that we understand which feelings and actions are our responsibility and which are not. People influence one another, but *influence is different than control.*

If I'm running down the street and decide to punch someone in the face, that's my responsibility. (I confess I used to think this was hilarious to do in *Grand Theft Auto*.) If that person decides they are going to pull out a gun and shoot me, they can be convicted of murder. This person could defend themselves by saying, "They hit me so they made me do it!" My choice to hit them was clearly wrong and I am responsible for that. However, this doesn't mean I am to blame for their response. I don't control them or how they choose to respond to my action.

People affect one another. This is a simple truth. And people experience sexual attraction to others. This attraction can definitely be triggered by seeing a person. Sexual attraction is certainly a strong force. The desire we can feel for another person can be one of the strongest feelings we ever experience. Yet no one else can control us more than ourselves.

Unfortunately, many times people have claimed, "I couldn't help myself!" in regards to their sexual desires. This is part of the notion behind the concept of so-called "rape culture." Men have been most likely to make these claims. And too many people have believed that "boys will be boys," meaning that men can't control themselves.

Let's be clear: A man can feel sexual desire no matter how much a woman is covered. A man can feel sexual desire just thinking about a woman without one even being present. Certainly we can't blame all of men's sexual desire on women's immodesty.

As we go through life, numerous events will trigger feelings and emotions. Or sometimes we feel these for apparently no reason at all. Regardless, *we are responsible for handling our subsequent actions.*

We instinctively look to blame something or someone besides ourselves. So it's not surprising that men would point to women as the source of their sexual attraction. From a man's perspective, it makes some sense. "I saw a woman, found her attractive, now I'm experiencing sexual desire." It's a short leap from this to "She caused my attraction." From this perspective, it's understandable why modesty has often been required of women. However, it is wrong to shift the responsibility of men's sexuality from them to women. Despite it being understandable why a man would blame a woman, it's ultimately *his responsibility*—not hers.

One quality I've noticed about women is that when something goes wrong, many question themselves first. It's good to not immediately jump to blame others. Yet the downside is that women often take too much responsibility on themselves.

Someone may wonder, "Are women not responsible at all for what they wear?" No. What I am saying is that even if a supermodel walks naked down the street, I (as a man) am not justified in sexually assaulting her. No one else controls me more than I do myself, and therefore I am responsible for my own actions.

It's often been said that men are visual and women are relational. It may be true that men tend to be more visually stimulated while women tend to be more influenced by feelings of intimacy. But it's important we don't take this too far. It's not that all men are only sexually stimulated by seeing women or that all women are 100 percent unstimulated by seeing an attractive man. Not all men and not all women are wired exactly the same way. Even the most typical woman can be turned on by seeing a hot guy, and conversely, relationships are important to many if not most men.

While we don't control how others respond to us, it's good to know how we may impact others and to be considerate of them. Even if women tend to be less turned on by seeing men, I as a man shouldn't walk around naked any more than a woman should.

The Bible doesn't offer guidelines regarding modesty specifically tailored to the clothing in our culture. People love rules, and many will try to create them when they are lacking. However, no standards for modesty are universally agreed upon among all Christians. I mean, we generally agree it's not appropriate to go around naked or in one's underwear, and that swimwear is appropriate only at the pool or beach. But beyond this, it's difficult to say anything definitive. As with other subjects in the New Testament, we must walk by the Spirit and use discernment to determine the best way to present ourselves as opposed to seeking rigid rules.

Based on what I've heard from Christian women, they feel they are in a tricky situation. On the one hand, they traditionally aren't supposed to initiate a relationship with a man. Instead, they feel the need to be attractive—both physically and otherwise—in hopes of having a man become interested enough to initiate a relationship with them himself. And, of course, they hope to be attractive enough to capture the interest of the best men. On the other hand, modesty tells women that it's their fault if men are sexually attracted to them.

Imagine a woman is preparing to go to church. She has a dress she loves and feels beautiful in. But what might she feel a need to debate in her head? What if it shows her shoulders? Ankles? Knees? *Gasp* Her legs? Back? Heaven forbid the dress reveal any cleavage! But what if it merely reveals the shape of her breasts? Is that appropriate? Or somehow sinful? As a man, I've never had to consider these questions.

I can imagine this would be maddening and anxiety inducing. Unfortunately, I've heard it's often women who criticize other women the most. Even worse, young ladies may be unaware of all of the "rules" other people have. A teenage girl may dress without knowing what other people think of certain clothing. She may wear something that isn't inappropriate yet end up having other women criticize her. Once a woman is well-established in her own beliefs, she can brush off those people who hold a differing view. But young women in this position frequently aren't yet settled in their beliefs and self-confidence. Criticism they receive regarding their dress, especially when it is really not inappropriate, may result in them feeling ashamed of their own body.

Because modesty is very gender imbalanced, women often internalize the overarching message that they should be ashamed to be women, to have breasts and butts and curves. They should cover these up as much as possible, almost so as to become neutered.

Evangelicals tend to be afraid of bodies in large part because we're afraid of sex. And we're afraid of sex because we've blown the consequences out of proportion to reality.

* * *

Purity culture idolized the concept of purity. Out of a fear of teen sex and potential consequences, Christian leaders attempted to scare the sex out of teens. But the fear led to unintentional messages that deeply impacted many of the most devoted youth, especially girls, with long-lasting consequences. One of these unintentional messages was that if "purity" was "lost," it could never be fully regained and the person was forever significantly deficient and unworthy. All of this led to unhealthy shame regarding one's own body and sexuality. However, these messages are antithetical to the good news of Jesus.

XXX

"I beg you to let the man of God you sent to us come again to teach us how to bring up the boy who is to be born." Judges 13:8

"Instruct the wise and they will be wiser still; teach the righteous and they will add to their learning." Proverbs 9:9

In the previous chapter, we looked at evangelicalism's relationship with sex. We learned about the evangelical fear of sex and the problems with the pursuit of purity. In this chapter, we'll learn more about positive teaching regarding sex.

Some Christians have feared to teach on the subject lest people be triggered to engage in sex in what they fear will be an immoral way. But only teaching the Bible's prohibitions regarding sex has led to an imbalanced message. It has left many believers ignorant of basic information necessary to successfully navigate life.

I've long heard that sexuality is about more than just the act of sex.[24] Christianity didn't teach me about anything else, though, nor did my parents. Part of what it means to be a sexual person—even if I am not married (I, the author, am not)—is that I have sexual parts, I have a gender, I desire relationships and intimacy. These things listed above are something that any person should be taught growing up and be aware of by the time they are somewhere in their teenage years.

Much of this isn't taught directly in the Bible. The transfer of knowledge was presumed. While I understand the sentiment behind the analogy, the Bible wasn't designed to be a comprehensive manual for life—even though it does contain a great amount of wisdom for life. In relation to our current discussion, no book and chapter in the Bible spells out healthy sexuality. Despite this, part of teaching sexuality involves not only teaching what is unhealthy and wrong but also what is healthy and good.

When we don't teach a balanced and healthy understanding of sexuality, this leads to a number of problems. First, some people don't learn how to engage others of the opposite sex and never develop healthy relationships that lead to marriage. For example, Thomas Umstead Jr. was a long time promoter of courtship.[25] Yet after many years he began to recognize that many who pursued this approach did not end up married. He ended up changing his paradigm and, as a result, got married not too long after. He wrote a book called *Courtship in Crisis* which I found very helpful in my own journey of learning.

As mentioned in the previous chapter on purity culture, there are good reasons for wanting teens to abstain from sex. However, it didn't provide additional appropriate guidance as people became young adults. This left many of those who grew up as teens in purity culture unprepared to handle the world of adult relationships.

Along with this, many Christian couples, when they do get married, struggle with sex. If a person has been told over and over for years that sex is effectively bad, this belief doesn't flip over night once they've spoken their wedding vows. One may consciously think that sex should be acceptable and good. But because of the heavy emphasis on purity, one's body and subconscious can still protest. For example, a woman may experience a painful spasm of related muscles during intercourse. This is treatable (discuss with your doctor), but it something that is good for Christian couples to be aware of as a possibility ahead of time.[26]

Additionally, Christian couples' expectations may be too high. They may have received the message that marital sex will always be pure bliss from the wedding night on, which can lead to disappointment and subsequently conflict in their marriage. They may be more likely to think there is something wrong with themselves or their spouse instead of recognizing that their expectations were unrealistic.

All these point to the need for healthy, godly teaching on sexuality and interrelated topics. The truth is most people experience sexual desire. This isn't wrong or bad. This is how God created us. The first command in the Bible is to be fruitful and multiply—and we're not talking about doing math here!

It's natural for us to be curious about our sexuality. We wonder what people's anatomy looks like. What is the range of shapes and sizes? What is "normal"? Are my parts normal? Am I big, small, average? How do these parts work? Are my desires normal and healthy or are they "bad"? Are the changes in these parts normal? What should I do when I experience __? What do I do with the feelings I have? What is the right way for people to interact when physical attraction is present?

Unfortunately, due to the evangelical fear of sex, Christians have historically provided little information regarding all of these aspects of sexuality. Even more unfortunately, Christians have too often tried to restrict what anyone, Christian or not, can teach regarding sexuality, often limiting it to abstinence. Once again, this has contributed to sexual problems both in Christianity and our culture at large. Sexuality promiscuity is not the only path to sexual problems.

With our natural curiosity but little information, many people—including Christians—have turned to pornography to learn about sex. It should go without saying that porn isn't designed as a healthy, accurate, or comprehensive sex education. It does a poor job at this task. Yet the solution isn't to vilify porn for this reason so much as it is to replace its poor lessons with good, healthy sex teaching. Or in other words, regardless of what we think about and teach regarding porn, we need to have good, healthy teaching about sexuality.

Comprehensive sex education could be an entire book. As such, a full treatment of the subject is well beyond the scope of this chapter. The purpose of this chapter is to share a brief overview of the topics involved.

Parents feel ashamed to talk about sex as a result of it being taboo. This is so well known that we have probably all heard of the painfully awkward "talk" about the "birds and the bees." However, I once heard someone say that teaching your kids about sex shouldn't be a single hour-long monologue given once. Instead, good teaching about sexuality takes place over numerous minute-long conversations through a child's life.

As Christians, we may hold some aspects of sexuality to be immoral. We may oppose abortion, for example. But we need to teach our children what these things are rather than not teaching about them at all. If we don't, they will learn about it elsewhere. As we teach our children, we have an opportunity to explain to them our views and values on these matters.

I recently learned about what are called the circles of sexuality. Each of these (save for one) has a scope that is broader than just the act of sex. Nevertheless, they play an important role in sexuality. I'm going to share these, each under its own subheading, in terms of teaching children as they grow. Clearly, though, we can still learn as adults those things that we were not taught ourselves growing up.

Biology, Anatomy, and Sexual/Reproductive Health

First of all, children learn early on that there are boys and girls. They also learn about their own body, including their sexual organs. Children need to be taught about how there are different sexes in plants, animals, and people. At a younger age, they need to be taught regarding how to care for their own bodies. At a bit of an older age, they should be taught more about the anatomy of the opposite sex. Along with this, they need to be taught what is appropriate in regards to clothing and touch.

There are physical changes which happen during a person's life, most notably at puberty. A child should be informed about the kind of changes to expect and be helped through these when they happen. Girls, for instance, will better cope with their monthly cycle if adults come alongside them with information and support.

Furthermore, children need to be taught at an appropriate age about the act of sexual intercourse and how this can potentially lead to pregnancy. We need to teach about pregnancy and child birth. STIs, contraception, and abortion are also subjects that older children should be taught.

Gender

The previous "circle" related to the physical parts that make one male or female, as well as the biology of reproduction. Traditionally, no distinction has been made between sex and gender, and more often than not these do correspond. Gender has to do with the *concepts* of what it means to be a man or a woman, masculine or feminine. Gender considers what it means to be a man or a woman, evaluating the typical cultural expectations for each gender.

Many Christians prefer traditional gender roles. This brings to mind the image of a man who works outside of the home, earning an income to provide for his family financially. When he comes home, his expected duties include the more physical work of home maintenance. A woman, on the other hand, performs more of the household chores, such as cooking and cleaning. Women generally handle the burden of child rearing as well. In a nutshell, the husband is expected/required to be the provider (specifically financially) while the wife is expected/required to take care of the domestic duties.

However, the Bible does not teach these strict roles for men and women. The roles we see as traditional are actually more an idealization of mid-twentieth century America. This vision clings to the image of a clean-cut white family in the age before rock music, the sexual revolution, civil rights, and other progressive movements which took place during the 1960s.

If you are a Christian who prefers traditional gender roles like this, by all means, follow this path with godly exuberance. However, some couples have found they are poorly suited to traditional gender roles. This is fine as well. I've heard at least one pastor condemn as sin when a man stays home with his kids while his wife works. This notion is ridiculous. How often have Christians encouraged men to be better fathers? How often have we been concerned about absent or disengaged fathers? Which is actually more godly: a man who pays for his family's expenses but is otherwise disengaged, or a man who works hard caring for his kids and taking care of the family home but who doesn't happen to have a paycheck at the time? Life is sometimes complicated and doesn't go according to plan. Some families find themselves in a position in which the man is out of employment while the wife is employed. No condemnation here. A couple should do what works best for them, their marriage, and the situation they find themselves in. It is an honorable job for a man to raise children. To say otherwise would admit that the work deemed as "women's" holds less value. In reality, women are every bit as valuable as men and the work of the former as valuable as that of the latter.

The only sin in regards to gender roles is to judge—to condemn others for being different from you and your ideals. God has created all men and all women, and he has not created us all the same. We sin when we criticize God's work by saying that a person he has created is not a "real" man or a "real" woman.

The topic of sexual orientation is also included in the gender "circle." Though many Christians believe that proper sex only takes place between a man and woman, a child at the appropriate age also should be aware that some people experience attraction toward people who are the same sex as themselves (homosexual), for anyone (bisexual), or for no one (asexual).

Relationships/Intimacy

First, understand that intimacy means more than just sex, even though the word is often used this way. Intimacy is relational closeness. Physical intimacy generally refers to sex and related activities. But one can also have emotionally intimate relationships. And these aren't limited to a spouse. We can (and probably should) have close friends and/or family members with whom we can share our deep thoughts and desires. An aspect of our humanity is that we desire to connect with other people, to have relationships with them, to love and be loved.

For this "circle," we want to teach children about the different types of relationships we may have through our lives. We should teach what healthy relationships look like and the kinds of things that are appropriate and inappropriate to share based on the relationship. Teaching boundaries is also crucial, as is identifying and avoiding unhealthy relational dynamics, such as codependency and abuse. Kids need to learn healthy ways to handle conflict and emotions. They must learn how to identify safe and unsafe people as well.

Sensuality

Sensuality has to do with pleasure and what stimulates our senses in a pleasing way. It involves more than just sex, though sexual stimulation is one of these pleasures.

We may experience various sights, sounds, smells, tastes, and touches as pleasant and enjoyable or repulsive and painful. Some of these are common to most people, such as finding flowers pleasing and poop disgusting. That said, our personal preferences are subjective.

Again, sensuality goes beyond sexuality, though it is a part of it as well. God has made sexual intimacy sensual and pleasurable. He clearly desires us to enjoy this intimacy with our spouse.

People have different preferences in regards to how they enjoy sex. It will be difficult for a partner to know what these are without communicating with one another. It can take time to learn one's own likes and dislikes, and that's OK.

In relation to this "circle," it is also good to consider how we feel about our bodies. This subject is especially important to discuss with girls as culture places a significant focus on women's bodies. We can discuss what it means to inhabit one's body and the importance of caring for it. It is important to learn to be kind to one's body, something many of us struggle with.

Sexualization

This "circle" relates to sexually engaging with others in a way that may lead to romance, dating, marriage, and sex. In other words, we need to answer the question of how we interact with a person who is a stranger and attempt to progress a relationship toward a potential lifelong partnership.

Teens need to be taught about flirting, sexual attractiveness and what behaviors are appropriate with the opposite sex. What kinds of clothing are appropriate and inappropriate? Is it acceptable to draw attention to one's self and one's body? When is it OK to flirt? What kinds of flirting are acceptable and unacceptable? How does one turn down unwanted advances? What do we do if someone we like also likes us? What kind of dating or romantic relationships are appropriate at different ages? When could I consider marriage? What should I require in a potential spouse? How do I know I should get engaged or break off a relationship? How should I break up with a partner?

Clearly, there is a lot to go over here. This is a great example of why sex shouldn't be a one-time conversation. How many of us would remember all of the answers if a parent told us once? Teens and young adults need ongoing guidance as they go through their own experiences.

In addition to teaching the appropriate ways of engaging with others, it is also important to teach which actions are wrong and harmful. We need to teach what constitutes unacceptable behaviors, such harassment and rape. *It is absolutely imperative to teach about consent,* which applies even in marriage.

A full exploration of marriage is beyond the scope of this book. However, I do want to say that many people have attempted to create a formula. If only a husband will do certain things and a wife certain other things, they say, then the marriage should work well. This can be especially true of Christians who suggest they are describing "biblical" and "godly" marriage.

The truth is there are many different kinds of people. Every relationship is therefore unique. Certainly, some universal rules exist, such as "a spouse should not cheat or be abusive." However, marriage requires a lot of flexibility. It's best and most effective for partners to figure out what works best for them. A couple can try prescriptions given by others, and if they work, great.

But they shouldn't feel obligated to a formula that doesn't work for them either.

Many people feel the need to hide certain experiences, such as struggles with sex in marriage. Other common difficulties include infertility, infidelity, miscarriage, abortion, arguments, and divorce. When people don't share these experiences, it makes these experiences seem more abnormal than they actually are. People who have gone through these negative experiences have talked about feeling alone. Yet my impression is these are all more common than what many of us realize.

We have healthy and unhealthy ways to share these experiences. Some of these shouldn't be shared widely on social media, for instance. Gossip—talking negatively about people who aren't present—isn't healthy, either. But each of us needs a community of close friends and family we can be open with, even about these difficult subjects.

* * *

Out of the fear of sex as well as a sense of taboo, Christians have not only *not* taught youth about healthy sexuality, but they have too often prevented others from teaching about sexuality as well. However, in order for Christians and their youth to live a fully healthy life as God intended as they become adults, they need to be taught a broad range of topics in regards to sexuality and relationships.

Bibliolatry

"For everything that was written in the past was written to teach us, so that through the endurance taught in the Scriptures and the encouragement they provide we might have hope." Romans 15:4

"Do not worship any god except me." Exodus 20:3 (CEV).

The Bible is God's word. It's the key document by which we know God's teachings. Without the Bible, we would be left with only tradition and people's own ideas of God. The Bible is important enough that we want to understand it correctly.

If the Bible is God's word, how could I possibly say there is any problem with it, any correction needed? I don't. The problem is not with the Bible; it's with us. Some Christians hold inaccurate beliefs regarding the Bible and conflate their beliefs about the Bible with the Bible itself.

Some have enshrined the Bible as a "sacred cow"—untouchable. As important as it is, it is possible to make so much of the Bible that it becomes an idol. In reality, it's not the Bible which people idolize; some Christians hold *their own beliefs about* the Bible as so holy that not even God himself could cause them to reconsider. Yet our faith shouldn't be in the Bible itself—our faith should be in Jesus.

Again, I'm not here to criticize the Bible. Instead, I want to help people understand the Bible better.

The Bible is a compilation of many different writings, composed by different authors, which took shape over the course of a couple thousand years. I've never heard anyone deny that the Bible was written by human beings. Yet the way evangelicals talk, many hold that God effectively possessed the human authors in order to write down exactly what he wanted, perfectly, word for word and without error.

You have likely heard of the concepts of biblical inerrancy or infallibility. For some, this actually does mean that every word in the Bible is without error in every way, including historically, chronologically, scientifically, etc. Other Christians believe the Bible is without error in its primary purpose of God's teachings but not necessarily in secondary matters.

The Bible is the most popular book of all time. More manuscripts of parts of the Bible exist than for any other ancient writing. As a consequence, the Bible also contains more discrepancies between manuscripts than for any other book. The vast majority of these discrepancies, called variants, are insignificant—obvious errors that are easily noted and corrected.

Some people who oppose Christianity point to the large number of variations and want to use this to suggest we have no idea what the original authors wrote. It's true we can't say for certain what the original manuscript said precisely character for character. But the suggestion that the original writing could therefore have said anything is simply not true. Some words or occasional passages are uncertain, but as a whole, what we have is close to the original.

In the present day, a book will go through many revisions and edits before it is published. Furthermore, a book may be republished in a new, updated edition. These concepts didn't exist in ancient times as they do now. Yet writings in ancient times could be edited and, unfortunately for us, this kind of editing and updating was not as clearly specified as it would be today. Ancient writings didn't come with a title page that included the author's name, nor was there a copyright date to clarify precisely when the writing was first "published."

We don't have the original copy of any of the books of the Bible. Even if we did, we would have no way of knowing it was the original manuscript. Therefore, the Bible is based on our best synthesis of all of the manuscripts we do have.

You may expect that the Bible has had the same importance throughout Christian history as it does to us today. But this isn't quite true. Up until the 1500s—and continuing today for Catholics—the church was the authority on Christianity.[27] Sure, the church had the Bible. But the expertise on Christianity was understood to reside in the church, comprised of ecclesiastic (church) leaders.

Once we take a moment to consider this, it makes sense. Before the printing press, the majority of people were illiterate. Books could only be copied by hand, which meant they were expensive. Imagine how long it would take someone to write out an entire copy of the Bible! This being the case, the church was the guardian, owner, and authority on the Bible.

With this in mind, we can understand why church leaders claimed to have direct, unbroken succession from Peter and the apostles. This was the basis for their claim of authority. In other words, someone could have asked, "How do we know the church is teaching correctly?" Their answer would be, "Because we received our teaching from the apostles who received it from Jesus, and we have handed down their teaching since then."

During the Reformation, one of Martin Luther's theses was "sola scriptura," or "scripture alone." (The Protestant Reformation would probably not have gotten off the ground had it not been for the printing press. The Reformers' ideas were spread through printing, and, just as importantly, the ability for mass production allowed the Bible to play a central role from here on out.)

The church arguably had strayed off course, evidenced in its promotion of the sale of indulgences, for instance. Luther suggested the authority for the Christian faith be moved from the church to the Bible. The Reformers emphasized the importance of the Bible, which we still see in Protestant Christianity today.

The Bible's newfound prominence had certain consequences. Now it was of upmost importance to know we could trust the Bible and know exactly what it said. Relying on the biblical text was a paradigm shift at the time. Before the Reformation, these questions regarding the Bible weren't as important. Minor variations in manuscripts were inconsequential because the church knew the correct teaching of Christianity. And Christians didn't need to know they could trust the Bible because they were expected to trust the church and its leaders.

You may have heard the phrase, "The Bible says it and that settles it!" This will normally be said to shut down a conversation regarding a topic on which the Bible teaches. The idea here is that since the Bible is written in plain English, its meaning is therefore straightforward and unquestionable.

This notion has some difficulties. First of all, language isn't meaning. Language is a code which encodes meaning. The language must be converted into meaning by the person reading it. I could open up a

Chinese Bible in front of you, point to a verse, and say, "See, the Bible says right here (fill in the blank); isn't it clear?" (I am assuming most of you reading this do not know Chinese.) Therefore, no matter how obvious and "black and white" the passage may be, it still has no meaning to you or me.

Why am I going into a philosophical monologue regarding language? Here's the thing: The Bible could be perfect in its original text. Yet we still have to read and *interpret* this text into meaning. During this process, differences can emerge between the author's original thought and our understanding.

If language communicates ideas imperfectly, does this subsequently mean the Bible could be saying anything at all? No, the latter doesn't follow from the former. Language has a generally agreed upon meaning; otherwise it would be completely meaningless! The fact that there are not absolute, mathematically precise meanings to a text only means that different people may take away different nuances to a text. In other words, a limited range of possible meaning exists rather than the extremes of either absolutely precise meaning or no meaning at all.

In addition to taking different nuances from a single text, people gather their understandings about God and his teachings from various parts of the Bible. The Bible is clearly a large book. With all of the different books and authors and genres, it's impossible to make a point using the entire text of the Bible at once. As we take a teaching from the Bible, we must consult some passages and not others. This isn't a problem so long as the conclusions gathered don't contradict other passages in the Bible.

Since most of us aren't reading the Bible in the original languages it was written in, it's worth spending some time exploring the topic of Bible translation in general and English translations in particular. Many Christians are baffled by the plethora of different English translations. If there is just one Bible, shouldn't there be one "correct" translation?

To understand translations, we first need to learn that more than one approach to translating between languages exists.

You may have heard the term *word-for-word translation*. This is a misleading and confusing term because there is no such thing as a word-for-word translation. For some concrete words, such as *table*, *book*, or *man*, there may be one–to–one correspondence between words in different languages. Table is *mesa* and man is *hombre* in Spanish, for example. However, many words do not have a one-to-one correspondence between languages, especially when dealing with more abstract concepts, such as judgment or love. We already saw in the chapter *Love Is a Verb* that our one English word *love* can be translated into Greek as one of several words, each with their own meaning.

It's also interesting to note there are only about 8,000 words in biblical Hebrew as opposed to the over 400,000 words we have in English.[28] This means that each Hebrew word can have a relatively wide range of meaning. An author can make use of this range of meaning in a beautiful way. But this can also mean more ambiguity and potential for different ways of understanding the text as well. Shalom is one such Hebrew word we saw in the chapter on hell.

These "word-for-word" translations are also referred to as "literal" translations, another misleading label. Technically, these Bible translations are not actually literal. Instead, they use the translation approach known as *formal equivalence*, the primary term I'll use for this translation approach from here on. (This could also be thought of as *structural* or *technical equivalence*, though I will stick to the common term.)

Not only do words frequently not have a one-to-one match in another language, the structure of sentences is often different in different languages as well. If one attempts to make an actual word-for-word translation, it's nearly unreadable. For example, here is a most literal translation of John 3:16:

> Thus for loved God the world that the son
> the only begotten he gave so that everyone
> believing in him not should perish but
> should have life eternal.

We can kind of get the message out of this translation since we are already familiar with this verse. But imagine trying to read the entire Bible this way! Even the strictest formally equivalent translations add words (such as articles and conjunctions) and rearrange words in order to make them more readable in English. For example, read John 3:16 again from the New American Standard Bible (NASB), considered the most strictly formally equivalent of English translations:

> For God so loved the world, that he gave his only Son, so that everyone who believes in him will not perish, but have eternal life.

So a formally equivalent translation actually means that the translators attempt to include the translation of each original word whether this results in one or more words. Strict formal equivalence also attempts to preserve the sentence structure as much as possible. However, formally equivalent English translations will rearrange words out of necessity in order to make a sentence readable in English.

Many people believe formally equivalent translations are more accurate and therefore better. But this is a misunderstanding that isn't necessarily true. The original authors of the Bible desired to communicate *ideas*, not just a series of words, to us. Consequently, a translation which attempts to communicate the meaning could actually be just as good if not a better translation.

The other most common translation approach is sometimes referred to as "thought-for-thought" translation. These translations attempt to convey the *meaning* of the text. To this end, they are less strict about each word. Technically, this approach is known as *dynamic* or *functional equivalence*. The goal is for the reader of the translation to receive a message that is *functionally equivalent* to the message a reader of the original language would receive.

The New Living Translation is a popular example of this translation paradigm.

> For this is how God loved the world:
> he gave his one and only Son, so that
> everyone who believes in him will not
> perish but have eternal life.

As you can see, though the NLT may be considered a "looser" translation, it is very close to the NASB and arguably every bit as accurate to the original text. Let's look at another example (from Romans 12:2) to better see a difference.

> And do not be conformed to this world,
> but be transformed by the renewing of
> your mind, so that you may prove what
> the will of God is, that which is good and
> acceptable and perfect (NASB).

> Don't copy the behavior and customs of
> this world, but let God transform you into
> a new person by changing the way you
> think. Then you will learn to know God's
> will for you, which is good and pleasing
> and perfect (NLT).

And from what is likely the newest English translation of the New Testament as of this writing:

> Don't conform to this world but be
> transformed by changing the way you
> think so that you'll be able to see
> what God's will is. His will is good,
> acceptable, and perfect. (The 21st Century
> New Testament)

A translation which is accurate but difficult to read is arguably not a great translation. Those translations which are easy to read in the most natural sounding modern English are suitable for the majority of people. Theologians, pastors, and scholars quibble about words here and there, but the differences aren't significant enough to argue against a translation's use by most Christians.

It's worth noting that the New Testament was originally written in common (*koine*) Greek. It was written in a manner just like people spoke, as opposed to sounding very formal and religious. Certainly part of the inspiration behind translations such as the New Living Translation and the 21st Century New Testament is to make the language of the Bible accessible to ordinary people. After all, it's better for people to have a Bible they read and understand than one don't read or don't understand.

Beyond the two translation approaches already discussed, some Bibles are considered paraphrases. Outside of the context of Bible translation, the term paraphrase means a person restates a previously written text in their own words. Functionally equivalent translations and paraphrases are often confused, and it may not be possible to define a strict line between them.

The Living Bible (not to be confused with the New Living Translation) is one example of a Bible which is *only* a paraphrase. It was not translated from the original languages but rather, a pastor used another English translation and reworded it into his Living Bible.

While some Bibles are only paraphrases, most Bibles that are considered paraphrases are actually translations. Yet because of the translation approach, one can consider them both a translation and a paraphrase. This is similar to functionally equivalent translation. The difference is that a paraphrase is looser in using idiomatic language. The translator first reads the original text, understands its meaning, then decides how he would communicate the ideas in his own words.

The Message is the best-known Bible on the paraphrase end of the translation spectrum.

> This is how much God loved the world: he gave his Son, his one and only Son. And this is why: so that no one need be destroyed; by believing in him, anyone can have a whole and lasting life (John 3:16).

> Don't become so well-adjusted to your culture that you fit into it without even thinking. Instead, fix your attention on God. You'll be changed from the inside out. Readily recognize what he wants from you, and quickly respond to it. Unlike the culture around you, always dragging you down to its level of immaturity, God brings the best out of you, develops well-formed maturity in you (Rom 12:2).

It's fair to consider The Message a paraphrase, yet it is still worth remembering that its author used the original Greek and Hebrew texts in its creation.

We have looked at the translation spectrum from formal equivalence to paraphrase. In reality, there are no major, strictly formally equivalent translations, and even paraphrases are based on what the Bible says, so no translation is fully divorced from the original text. Most translations sit somewhere between formal and functional equivalence. Some lean toward one side or the other, while still other translations attempt to find balance in the middle. The best known of the latter is the New International Version (NIV).

One perfect, or correct, or best English translation of the Bible does not exist. It's actually helpful to read a variety of translations.[29] Functionally equivalent translations are probably a better place to start for people who are new to reading the Bible. These are also good for devotional reading. The 21st Century New Testament is probably the easiest to read translation I've come across. On the other hand, a formally equivalent translation can be better when doing an in-depth, analytical study of a passage.

There are different ways to read the Bible and different purposes for doing so. One can study the Bible in an attempt to better understand it. One can read it devotionally. One can use it for prayer, encouragement, or meditation. One can sit and chew on a small portion of scripture or read a whole book, trying to understand the overall message. All of these reasons are valid, and different translations lend themselves better to each purpose. Reading from a different translation can bring a fresh perspective to the Bible and may bring out an angle that has been overlooked. And comparing translations can bring further insight.

Before I continue, I want to address a problem I have encountered more lately. It has become more common for pastors to talk about an underlying Greek or Hebrew word during a sermon on a passage of scripture. This practice can bring greater insight into the passage in question. However, some pastors have shared disagreements with the way a word was translated. The problem is this has led many people to the impression that most translations are poor or made with an agenda. I've been in many Bible studies in which a person will wonder what the underlying word is, assuming the meaning is somehow different than what has been translated. Here's the thing—Bible translators aren't stupid. The significant majority of the time, the word's meaning is exactly how it's translated.

* * *

Many Christians hold that the Bible has to be understood literally. It's easy to understand the logic. "If one part of the Bible isn't true, then none of it may be true." It's easier to hold that the Bible is all literally true and therefore straightforward, because one doesn't have to think any more about it after this. However, there aren't just two options: Either the Bible is literally true or it is not reliable at all.

There are a number of ways to resolve the tension. For example, we can understand that the Bible was written by human beings using their understanding of the natural world as they communicated God's truths. God knew that the sun is powered by a giant nuclear fusion reaction. Even so, it would have made no sense to say this in scripture because it would have been utterly incomprehensible to anyone prior to the mid-twentieth century. Every book in the Bible was written in a specific time and cultural context. The core teachings of the Bible may be true, but this doesn't require every contextual detail to be true as well.

The Bible is comprised of a variety of genres, and one of these is parable or story. This is another way in which the Bible isn't strictly true or false.

Does the year 2125 sound like a long way off? How about 3025? It's impossible to know what the world will be like. But imagine some people discover a copy of C.S. Lewis' *The Lion, the Witch, and the Wardrobe* in the year *6025*. They would be about as far in the future as the earliest parts of the Bible are in our past. The Bible is so familiar and accessible to us that it is easy to forget how old it is, especially the earlier parts of the Old Testament.

What might the future people think if they found this classic *Chronicles of Narnia* book? Might some of them be amazed that we thought talking animals led by a lion actually existed? They would imagine us silly, ignorant, and primitive for believing such. Perhaps others would think we had some knowledge that had subsequently been lost. "This shows that there were actually talking animals at one point!"

In reality, we all understand that *The Lion, the Witch, and the Wardrobe* is a piece of fiction that nonetheless contains an analogy to the real story of Jesus's sacrifice and resurrection through a fantasy world. If people in the far future do find *The Lion, the Witch, and the Wardrobe*, they will likely also have enough other information to ascertain our recognition of the book as fiction. But what if they did not?

You probably have heard the story of the boy who cried, "Wolf!" Suppose you shared this story with me and I asked, "What was the name of the town? What year did this take place? What was the boy's name?" You would probably inform me that I missed the point of the story. The point of the story is to communicate a true lesson, not that the story is true in itself.

Most Christians are aware that Jesus taught with parables, and I've never heard anyone argue these have to be literally true. Jesus shared a story about a man who was beaten and robbed and eventually rescued by a Samaritan (a.k.a. the story of "the good Samaritan"). What if I asked the same questions of this parable as I did of the story above? Wouldn't I also be missing the point? Do Jesus's parables have to be factually, historically true? They could be historical, but my question is, do they need to be?

What is your faith based upon? I stated at the beginning of the chapter that our faith ought to be built on Christ, not on a particular understanding of the Bible. Jesus doesn't stand on the Bible, and God would still exist even if there were no scriptures.

What belief do you hold that, if you found it to be untrue, would undermine your faith? For instance, what if we discovered that the tower of Babel was just a story? This might shock you, but would it undermine your faith? What if we discover that the Bible was a mix of divine and human input, and that some of what we read (especially in the Old Testament) was at times the author's incorrect views about God? Would this undermine Jesus?

Why do I bring this up? It's because many people have lost their faith over this sort of thing. They thought they had to believe in a literal worldwide flood, a literal seven-day creation, and take the rest of the first eleven chapters of Genesis literally in order to be a Christian. When they came to a point where they found they could no longer believe this, they then assumed they could no longer be a Christian at all.

We think those who are not Christians should become so, and those who are should remain so. My concern is that requiring people to believe in Genesis as literal history erects an unnecessary barrier to people's faith in Christ. I believe this is unnecessary for a couple of reason.

If Jesus was raised from the dead, does it matter if the world was created in six literal days? Maybe it was six thousand or six million years. If Jesus resurrected, then he is God and this verifies what he taught. None of the other beliefs and understandings about the rest of the Bible can nullify that fact. Or to restate it in another way, our faith should be in Jesus, not in a particular understanding of the Bible.

There is also a straightforward, easy to understand alternative to Genesis as literal history. It's possible that the earliest parts of Genesis were written as allegory. Many branches of Christianity view Genesis this way. Maybe the point is that God created, not in the details of how he did so. Maybe the point is that humanity was tempted and fell, not that there was literally a talking serpent. We can understand this part of Genesis as written to convey truths rather than the truths themselves. There are ample reasons for understanding Genesis in this way. I think the only reason this isn't clearer to us is that the allegorical nature of early Genesis has been lost over the thousands of years since it was written.

As time goes on, we learn more and more about the world. We also learn more about the Bible and the times in which it was written. Such background information is becoming increasingly accessible to a general audience. What once was available almost exclusively in the "ivory tower" of academia is becoming easy to access via the internet. At least some Christians are going to become more aware of these things. Much of this knowledge differs to some degree from that which has traditionally been held. If the church and its leaders deny the knowledge acquired by scholars and double down on their traditional beliefs, it will lead to more people leaving their faith unnecessarily. That which is brittle is most likely to break whereas resilience comes through a degree of flexibility.

* * *

Christians can idolize their understanding of the Bible above God himself. But our faith is to be in Jesus, not our understanding of the Bible. Our faith ought to be founded on Christ; the Bible isn't intended to bear this weight. If we stand on the firm foundation of Christ, we can hold onto the rest of our beliefs about the Bible with a looser grip, allowing other believers to hold different perspectives.

Epilogue

Thank you for taking the time to consider my words. Take a moment to unpack what you have read. Discuss ideas that moved or challenged you with some people you know.

- What idea(s) stuck out to you most?

- Which chapter or part of the book did you like most?

- What part(s) of the book did you find most challenging?

- In what ways has this book changed the way you see God?

- In what ways has this book changed the way you see yourself in relation to God?

- Is there anything you want or plan to change as a result of reading this book?

Most importantly, I hope you walk away with a better understanding of God's love, both what it is and isn't. I hope that what I wrote will relieve any worry about your salvation. I hope you will be able to move forward despite any fear that arises. I hope you will leave the worrying of others' behavior and salvation to God. I hope you will be able to show grace to others when they are in a different place in their spiritual journey than you are. I hope you will live in the healthiest experience of Christianity and help others to do the same. Together we can "cure" Christianity so that it is the light on the hill that Christ intended.

About the Author

Doug Webster, a.k.a. D. L. Webster, is an author, blogger, host of the *Digging Doug* podcast, and the bassist for rock band Rusty Shipp. He has spent most of his life involved in a handful of churches, first of all in his hometown of Indianapolis, then in his current residence in Nashville, TN. Most of these churches have been a part of the independent Christian Church branch of the Restoration or Stone–Campbell movement. He brings a wealth of knowledge gathered from years of sermons, teachings, and reading books, which he has synthesized together into this book. His passion is for Christians individually and the church as a whole to experience the healthiest approach to Christianity possible.

Endnotes

1. The New Testament was originally written in Greek.

2. This doesn't mean everything that happens is God's direct will. God's greater will is that people have free choice, and people often act against God's will.

3. From https://www.thegospelcoalition.org/what-is-the-gospel/ on 8/17/2023

4. That said, feeling angry is a completely appropriate response to abuse. Because of this anger, one may desire harm to this person. This feeling isn't wrong so long as one recognizes that this desire does not align with the person's humanity. Forgiveness is a process which doesn't happen in an instant, and it's ok to be in the middle of this process.

5. https://www.apa.org/topics/mental-health, 10/26/2025

6. Corresponding passages found in Matt 12:48–50 and Luke 8:21.

7. Credit to Dr. Paula Fredriksen for this phrase.

8. Greek tektōn

9. https://ahdictionary.com/word/search.html?q =hell

10. The period of time between the end of the Old Testament around 420 B.C. and beginning of the New around 4-5 B.C.

11. See also Mark 3:22–29, Luke 11:14–20.

12. The Last Battle, chapter 13, "How the Dwarfs Refused to be Taken In," C.S. Lewis.

13. Mark 1:14–15, Matt 4:23, 9:35, 11:5, Luke 4:43, 7:22, 8:1, 20:1

14. Though the phrase, "city on a hill" has been coopted to reference a certain view of the United States, I here invoke only the biblical meaning.

15. Gnosticism is a term which refers to a handful of early sects which shared certain aspects of

Christianity but were unorthodox.

16. Manicheism was a movement comprised of those who follow the teaching of a man named Mani, who attempted to meld ideas from various religions including Christianity.

17. Augustine held that sex was created by God, and that before the Fall, Adam and Eve were able to engage in sex dispassionately which was not sinful. But since the Fall, sex is effectively always sinful because it is always accompanied by desire, and Augustine believed this desire, "lust," to be sinful.

18. Brené Brown, The Gifts of Imperfection, (Minnesota: Hazelden, 2010), 41; Brené Brown, Daring Greatly, (New York: Gotham Books, 2012), 71

19. These were suggestions made to Christians to avoid lust.

20. Tina Schermer Sellers, Sex, God & the Conservative Church, (New York: Routledge, 2017), 17.

21. "Unless you're so drunk that you can't remember it, there's no such thing as casual sex because the brain is always responding." https://www.1440.org/blog/casual-sex-is-neve

r-casual-what-the-brain-reveals 05/27/2024 as well her stating similar in videos.

22. In the book, The Scarlet Letter, the main character is shunned for becoming pregnant out of wedlock. However, no one in the town knows who the father is, so he as the man escapes the same consequences.

23. From https://spsp.org/news/character-and-context-blog/friese-gender-differences-sex-drive 3/23/2025.

24. One example: Lisa Graham McMinn, Sexuality and Holy Longing, (San Francisco, Jossey-Bass, 2004), 69.

25. Courtship was a paradigm of how to get to marriage that was popular among some on the more conservative side of purity culture. The idea was that men and women would be kept at a physical and relational distance unless they decided to pursue marriage with one another. There was more to it, but this effectively meant that people would need to decide who they wanted to marry before they started a relationship! It's no wonder this paradigm led to fewer marriages.

26. https://www.facebook.com/JayStringerUnwan
ted/posts/pfbid02tNhWSPSbR2M8SB6savkcK
Fgs9sMAGBWJEQgbRKouiJUV8RVcVmz5xLrce
a7R5hNkl

27. In this section, when I refer to "the church," I
am speaking of the Roman Catholic Church as
a whole. Before Protestantism, there was only
one church denomination in the West.

28. Walking in the Dust of Rabbi Jesus, Lois
Tverberg, p. 36.

29. I have written an article which gives an
overview of the major English translations
which can be found on my website,
http://www.dlwebster.com